DEER

BLANDFORD MAMMAL SERIES
Advisory editor: Ernest G. Neal M.B.E., M.Sc., Ph.D., F.I.Biol.

DEER
Raymond E. Chaplin

BADGERS
Ernest G. Neal

DEER

RAYMOND E. CHAPLIN

B.Sc., M.I.Biol.

BLANDFORD PRESS

POOLE   DORSET

First published 1977 *Blandford Press Ltd.*
Link House, West Street
Poole, Dorset BH15 1LL

ISBN 0 7137 0 796 8

Printed in Great Britain by
Butler & Tanner Ltd., Frome and London

Colour plates printed by
Sackville Press Billericay Ltd., Billericay, Essex

Contents

Illustrations

Most of the illustrations in the book—line drawings, black and white photographs and colour plates—were provided by Raymond E. Chaplin/Netherfield Visual Productions.

Other sources, which the author and publishers gratefully acknowledge, are listed below.

Black and white photographs

K. R. Duff and Roy A. Harris: Figs 2.2, 3.4, 6.4, 7.8, 8.6, 8.7 and 12.1
A. W. Banfield/National Museum of Canada: Fig. 1.3
Tom Willock/Ardea Photographics: Fig. 5.2
Edgar Jones/Ardea Photographics: Fig. 6.7
S. O. Mann/Rowett Research Institute: Figs 7.4 and 7.5
Meridian Air Maps Ltd: Fig. 6.1(b)
W. Newlands/Highland Wildlife Park: Fig. 12.2

Colour plates

Phillipa Scott/NHPA: 4
Geoffrey Kinns: 5
George Schaller/Bruce Coleman Ltd: 12
E. H. Rao/NHPA: 17
Roberto Bunge/Ardea Photographics: 21
Joe Van Wormer/Bruce Coleman Ltd: 22
John Willet: 25

Acknowledgements

It would not have been possible to write this book without the assistance of a great many people all over the world. I have drawn freely on their published reports and papers but it has only been possible to make specific reference to a few of these here. To have done otherwise, would have resulted in a text so heavily cluttered with citations that it would have been unreadable. To all of these workers I express my thanks.

Over the years many organisations and people have assisted with my own research and I am especially grateful to the following organisations. Research funds were provided by the Royal Society for a study of reproduction in Roe deer and by the Natural Environment Research Council for an investigation of the biology of native and alien deer in Britain. This latter grant to Professor R. J. Harrison enabled me to work on this programme from the Anatomy School of Cambridge University. Additional research facilities and support were provided by their Graces, the Duke and Duchess of Bedford at Woburn Abbey; the Zoological Society of London at Whipsnade Zoo; the Forestry Commission, the Passmore Edwards Museum, Newham; the Superintendent of Richmond Park, Surrey; the Superintendent of Epping Forest; the Royal Zoological Society of Scotland; the Wildlife Breeding Centre, Wheathamstead.

My special thanks are due to Professor R. J. Harrison for his help and encouragement over many years, and to Dennis Talbot at Woburn for his enthusiastic support and practical help in my studies there. Many other people have been of great assistance to me and I would especially like to thank Group Captain W. Maydwell, Richard Prior, the late Kenneth Marshall, John Wilson, Bill Grant, Colonel J. Cockburn, David Davis, P. Fontaine, V. J. Manton, D. Jones, Duff Hart Davis, Professor K. Mellanby,

Alan Frost, H. B. Bird, G. McReddie, F. Kennedy, J. Cubbie, Mrs. A. Francis, R. W. G. White, Jennie Coy, D. I. and N. Chapman, Dr. P. Bramley, John Atkinson, Graham Dangerfield, R. Rose, Dr. B. A. Young, Dr. H. Frädrich, Dr. J. M. Dolan, Jr. and Dr. D. C. Thomas. Within the Forestry Commission I would especially like to thank the regional Conservators and all their staff in England and Scotland who went to so much trouble to collect and record specimens and data for me. I would also like to thank the staff of the Anatomy School, Cambridge University, for their skilled help and support.

I am grateful to Dr. Colin Holloway of the International Union for the Conservation of Nature and Natural Resources and to the British Deer Society for allowing me to reproduce an updated version of his paper on Endangered Deer which first appeared in the journal *Deer*. I also thank those who have given permission for the reproduction of their photographs and for the redrawing of maps, tables etc. and to Professor R. Short for the loan of the antler potion shown in Fig. 1.4. Specific acknowledgement for these is made on page vi.

Finally my special thanks to my wife and children for their help and encouragement.

Preface

It has been my privilege over the last fifteen years to have been able to observe and study many of the world's deer at first hand and to read and research the literature about them. As a book, *Deer* is a synthesis and personal distillation of a part of this experience which I hope will both stimulate and inform others about these fascinating animals. Deer and other wildlife all over the world need our urgent protection and I hope that readers of this book will give their support to the Endangered Deer Programme and other work of the IUCN which is funded by the World Wildlife Fund.

Raymond E. Chaplin
Galashiels, 1977

1 Deer and their World

The word 'deer' conjures up many different impressions, depending on who you are and where you live, and stirs many different emotions. To some it is the pleasure of watching one of nature's most elegant animals, to others the excitement of hunting an elusive creature, or maybe the anger of farmers or foresters as they survey the remains of their crop. In another area of the world it is just another jungle animal that will fetch a good price in the restaurants of the nearest city.

Deer of one kind or another are found in most parts of the world, some are large, others small, some solitary, others gregarious. The great variety of the deer and their distribution in very different places makes them a fascinating study. Almost all the great problems faced by wildlife today are exemplified within the deer family—the Cervidae.

The complex relationship between the biology and behaviour of each species and its environment is the climax of tens of thousands of years of evolution. Evolution is a dynamic and continuing process and the selective pressures for the survival of the species are now more intense than ever before. The future of many of our deer is going to depend on specific acts of conservation which will require a close knowledge and understanding of the species concerned.

There are 40 or so species of deer living today and these are found in habitats ranging from tropical forests to Arctic tundra. Deer are indigenous to Europe and Asia and both North and South America, but they are not found in Africa south of the Sahara nor in the Australasian region (Australia, New Zealand and adjacent islands). During the last century some eight species of deer were liberated in New Zealand and several species have also been introduced to Australia and some of the Pacific islands.

The majority of these have established themselves successfully in the wild.

On a number of occasions the deer of one region have been introduced to another part of the world and become part of the wildlife. In Britain, the Asian Reeves Muntjac, Sika, and Chinese Water deer live wild in many parts of the country. In South America, there are wild herds of imported Red and Fallow deer of European origin. Such introductions are, in most cases, detrimental to the wildlife which is already there. Often there is competition between the native and introduced species, or un-desired changes occur in the habitat. Too often the problems are only identified many years later. The impact of the European deer and other wildlife (which was brought to New Zealand in

Fig. 1.1 Adult Roe deer buck in winter coat showing the pale throat marks.

the nineteenth century) on the native flora and fauna can only be described as catastrophic and drastic measures against the new animals are now necessary to preserve the forest habitat.

Deer are closely related to antelopes and similar bovids (cattle, goats, yaks, bison, etc.). At first sight it can be difficult to be certain whether an unknown species is a deer or an antelope. The family Bovidae contains more species than the family Cervidae and are most numerous in Africa south of the Sahara. It is here that the evolving antelopes and their relatives expanded and diversified so that they are found in most areas and habitats. Antelopes were not so successful elsewhere. In Europe and Asia there are only a few members of the group and these highly specialised species

Fig. 1.2 Dense scrub woodland is an ideal habitat for the Reeves muntjac. This adult buck has recently cast its antlers and the new growth is just beginning.

such as the Chamois of the European Alps, the Blackbuck of India and the Chevrotains of the Malayan jungle are outnumbered by the variety of their bovid cousins (cattle, sheep, goats, bison, etc.) and by the deer.

There are many similarities in the morphology, physiology and biology of deer and antelopes. So much so that were we not here concerned with distinguishing between them we would normally emphasise the similarities. As described below, deer and antelopes share a common ancestor and the more primitive deer like Muntjacs closely resemble primitive antelopes such as the Maxwell's Duiker of the west African forests. One single feature however distinguishes the cervids from the bovids, namely the possession of antlers by male deer as opposed to horns by the bovids. In all species except two—the Chinese Water deer and Musk deer—the male has antlers. In only one species—the Reindeer—do both sexes normally have antlers. In all other species the occasional presence of antlers in the female is abnormal and is due to hormonal imbalance.

Antlers develop from a pair of short, bony columns called pedicles which are part of the frontal bone of the skull located above and behind the eye sockets. In most species antlers are first grown when the males are a year old, although in Roe and Reindeer the first antlers appear at about six months of age. The antlers are grown and then cast every year. On the other hand, horns are permanent, non-renewable structures. It is usual in the larger deer for the antlers to grow bigger and more complex in successive years, a process which continues up to maturity. Antlers are solid bone and are more fully described and discussed below.

In the bovids, horns may be present in one or both sexes and are fundamentally different from antlers. The horn has two parts— an inner core of bone which is normally largely hollow but of considerable strength, and the outer sheath. The bony core is a part of the occipital bone and is situated to the rear of the skull behind the ears. This core is covered by a sheath of keratin which is the true horn. Once fully formed the core does not grow further. The outer sheath has an annual cycle of growth which, in part, compensates for wear. In some species, such as male sheep, this

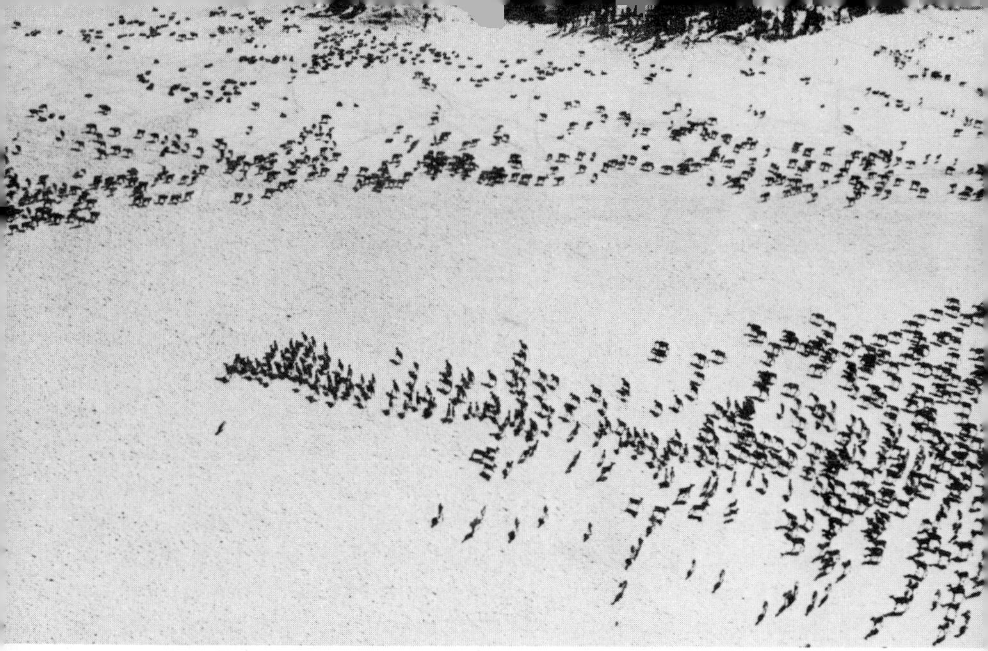

Fig. 1.3 Wolf chasing a herd of migrating Caribou Reindeer near Ghost Lake, North West Territories, Canada.

annual growth can be detected in the form of annual growth rings which may be counted in order to determine the approximate age of the animal. Neither the bony core nor the outer horn are ever cast, nor are they capable of substantial regeneration.

To the casual observer these are the only readily apparent features that separate the deer from the other families of ruminants. There are, however, a few anatomical features visible in the skull that also distinguish these groups and it is claimed that deer are the only ruminants to lack a gall bladder.

In the course of their evolution, deer are thought to have spread from central Asia in all directions so that they have colonised Europe, Asia and the Americas. They occupy most of the habitats that are found in these regions ranging from tropical forest to Arctic tundra. Typically, they are woodland dwellers, normally being found in cover rather than in more open country. However, this is probably a result of persecution by man rather than a specific need. Attempts at keeping species like Chinese Water deer and Roe deer in captivity suggest that, for these two at least, cover is a very important need. The former is capable of hiding satisfactorily in long grass, but the larger Roe requires the extra height of scrub or bramble. Others such as Red deer and

Fallow deer, both species that have long been kept in parks, do not however require such cover to flourish although it is used when available.

The most harsh environment occupied by deer is that of the Tundra and its woodland margins inhabited by the Reindeer. The Tundra is occupied seasonally as summer pasture. In Canada the Caribou (the Canadian Reindeer) migrate in spring several hundred miles into the Tundra to take advantage of the lush summer growth of the Arctic herbs and lichens and in autumn they return to the woodland margins. In northern Norway and Sweden, the mountain masses carry high level pastures above the tree line similar to those of the Tundra. In these areas the Reindeer with their herders may go high to these pastures in the spring, returning to lower ground often many miles away to survive through the winter.

The greatest number of species of deer are found within the sub-tropical woodlands and there are fewer in the cooler temperate regions with their seasonal environment.

The largest of the deer are the Moose (*Alces alces*—known as the Elk in Europe) and Wapiti (*Cervus canadensis*—known there as the Elk!) of Canada and the northern USA. These are larger than their close relatives in Europe. A full grown Moose may stand to about 2 m (6½ ft) at the shoulder and weigh around 600 kg (1,326 lb). The Wapiti may stand at about 1·5 m (5 ft) at the shoulder and weigh over 400 kg (883 lb). By contrast small deer such as the Reeves Muntjac stand at about 56 cm (22 in) and weigh around 12 kg (26½ lb) and some like the Pudu are smaller still. A similar degree of variation is found in the antelope family.

The abundance of the different species varies greatly. The largest numbers are found in those species with the most extensive areas of suitable habitat and among those with a plasticity that has enabled them to adapt to conditions over a very wide range. The population totals today are in most cases only a fraction of what they were a hundred years ago. Man alone is to blame for this. Our present picture may therefore be somewhat misleading in detail because it is the product of a very recent and artificial situation. Nevertheless, it is now the real situation and it is against this background that most important conservation and management decisions will be taken.

The Reindeer or Caribou of the north lands have a circumpolar population approaching a million animals. In the USA, where wildlife resources are monitored over the whole country, firmer estimates of game populations are available. There the population of Mule deer and White Tailed deer are of the order of three million and eight million, respectively. With its Eurasian distribution the Roe deer population must be well in excess of a million animals. For many species we cannot be precise about numbers. Census work on a wily animal in dense cover even in a small wood can take months and still be out by a factor of 2 or 3. Thus, for many species like the forest Muntjacs of Asia and the Brockets of South America, we have no idea of numbers nor do we often know their status or distribution in any detail. For some species our lack of knowledge is due to a lack of animals, even if we cannot be precise we know that there are very few. The Sika deer of Formosa is probably extinct as almost are other island races of this species. Sub-species of the Red deer, like the Hangul, are also severely depleted and numbered in tens or occasionally hundreds. The little Kuhl's deer of Bawean island is found only on that island and there is a breeding group in the Djakarta Zoo. Some depleted species can be closely monitored. For species like the Pere David, which is extinct in the wild, it is simply a matter of checking the World Register published in the International Zoo Year Book.

In their homelands the deer are a large part of the biological production. For this reason they are natural subjects for human utilisation or management. Later we shall see how this productivity has been utilised and how it may be expanded in the future. It is the Reindeer that made possible the traditional way of life of the Lapplander and there are no other species of domestic animal that makes such an efficient and productive use of the northern habitat. In the USSR several species of deer are farmed, not for meat but for their antlers at various stages of growth. Antlers and other parts of deer are a highly regarded part of many traditional oriental medicines and potions.

By tradition, deer are generally said to be browsers rather than grazers. This distinction between animals that primarily graze the low growing ground plants and those that supplement this by browsing leaves from trees and bushes only holds true where the

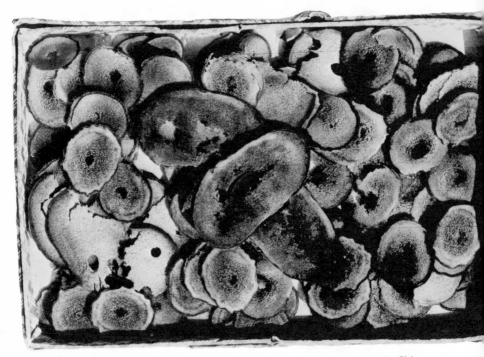

Fig. 1.4 Deer antler as offered for sale for medicinal purposes in China. In the Far East deer antler has been used for many centuries as the basis of various tonics. The growing antler is removed from the live deer, cut into thin slices and dried. The tonics may be prepared from this either by grinding into a powder or by solvent extraction. The medicinal value, if any, of these potions is not known.

animals are living on open grassland or mixed habitat areas. Given the chance most grazers will browse and all browsers, including giraffes, graze. Both deer and antelope have a very similar feeding apparatus and both are ruminants, that is they chew the cud. There are no upper teeth in the front of the mouth as in horses and humans. Instead eight chisel-like teeth work against an upper gum-like pad. Often a twig will be bitten three quarters through and then torn away. This leaves a characteristic scar that enables the forester to distinguish between damage done by hares and rabbits and that done by deer. When feeding, deer rarely chew what they have taken. A few strokes from the cheek teeth (molars and premolars) to break it up and the mouthful is swallowed. The stomach of ruminants has four chambers and the food first passes into the largest of these—the rumen/ reticulum. When this is full the animal finds a secluded spot and begins to cud. The food passes in small lumps back to the mouth where it is thoroughly chewed and is again swallowed, passing this time into a different chamber and thence through the gut.

The ruminant system has considerable advantages in terms of survival. A horse, which is not a ruminant, has only a small stomach and must fully chew all its food before swallowing. It therefore spends the greater part of the day and night feeding. The ruminant, however, is collecting food for very much shorter periods. In summer perhaps only one hour in five or six is actually spent gathering food, the chewing of the food occurring at leisure in a suitable spot. The survival value of such a process is very apparent and its success over the alternatives is made clear by the fact that nearly all the large hoofed herbivores of grassland and forest are cud chewers.

In captivity the diet of deer is by no means uniform. There are some that will take a wide range of alternative diets, such as oats, maize or commercially made pellets. However, some do not thrive without some natural food to supplement the basic rations. Roe deer, especially if they have not been hand-reared, require regular amounts of assorted wild plants and leaves to keep them fit and Reindeer seem unable to flourish without substantial quantities of their natural food, the lichen *Cladonia rangiferina*. This really emphasises the point that although many species have a broad spectrum of adaptability to different food sources, some have become physiologically specialised to a much narrower range of foods. What the particular essential ingredients are, is not known. These specialisations have produced some unusual feeding patterns and also some unexpected dangers. Moose are very fond of succulent water plants and will dive to depths of around 10 m (33 ft) and remain submerged for nearly a minute to get at the plants. At such times the animals are at risk to under-water obstacles and currents which might trap them and to the approach of a hunter. This vulnerability when in the water has been used to good effect by biologists studying both Moose and Reindeer. Animals captured as they swim lakes and rivers are readily tagged, examined and released.

Reindeer are affected in a more subtle and insidious way. Lichens,

9

which are a main part of their diet, absorb and concentrate radio-active substances such as strontium 90, which is then passed on in greater concentrations in the milk to the young to be incorpor-ated in the skeletal tissues. A known health hazard in humans, its effect on the Reindeer is not known with any certainty. Whether this can become concentrated to lethal levels in the human and wolf predators remains to be disclosed.

Increasing concentrations of persistent chemicals along food chains is very well known. Deer as consumers of plants are in the middle position of a short food chain and are not known to have been directly affected on any scale by the use of insecticides and herbicides. Equally, concentrations of substances like DDT now present in almost all living creatures are not known to have reached levels in deer where their flesh would have constituted a health hazard.

Man shares with deer the basic senses of sight, hearing, smell and touch but there is a great deal of difference in the use and degree of development of these between the two. The most developed of the deer's senses are those of smell and hearing. In a forest situation it is by reading the chemical messages (smells) carried by the air currents that deer are able to detect events for a considerable distance up wind. Downwind, or on a still day, the deer depend on their hearing to detect an intruder and an alerted deer can be seen to move its ears like a pair of radar dish aerials to obtain a fix on a sound and enable the eyes to make a visual contact, meanwhile the moist nose twitches seeking chemical identification.

The visual acuity of deer is both good and bad. Deer readily detect movement and also contrasts, alien shapes and tones—but if carefully camouflaged it is quite easy to avoid visual detection by deer even if they have been alerted by noise. Deer are well endowed with scent glands and these provide a multitude of odours that are dispersed in many different ways. The reading of these probably makes conversation superfluous! But in any case there are both auditory and visual reinforcements in the form of say thrashed bushes liberally anointed with scent from glands of the forehead (e.g. Roe, Muntjac). A rutting stag not only smells of rut, even to a human, but loudly advertises the fact by roaring, grunting or shrieking, depending on the species.

Fig. 1.5   Adult male Chinese Water deer, in winter coat, showing alertness.

The voices of deer are not well known and it is difficult to guess at the significance and extent of vocal communication outside of certain clear cut categories, e.g. the rutting calls, alarm signals and distress cries of the young. This is a subject where a great deal of work needs to be done and with fairly sophisticated equipment if we are to detect at a distance the barely audible chatter that appears to go on in groups of species like Red and Fallow.

The study of deer is a fascinating and rewarding activity that is available to many of us. The insights into the lives of these animals requires both simple and complex techniques and thus provides many opportunities for individuals or groups to contribute to our knowledge. The scent marking of territories for example can be studied by direct observation of when and how the scent is applied, whilst chemical analysis of the scent applied (collected by swabbing) requires the skills of the analytical chemist to characterise them. The world of deer, even of those on our doorsteps, is still largely unexplored and provides biologists with a major challenge.

2 Names and the Future

There are two ways of naming an animal. You can either call it by whatever name you think is most suitable and accept that others will do the same, or you can use the internationally accepted system of scientific names. In the latter system, every living organism has a unique double-barrelled name nominated by the first person to publish a full description. This name has two parts, the generic name and the specific name. For the Reeves Muntjac *Muntiacus reevesi*—*Muntiacus* is the generic name and *reevesi* the specific name. They work rather like a surname and christian name. The generic name is the equivalent of the surname. The scientific name identifies the animal and shows its relationship with other similar animals. There are, for example, five species of Muntjac deer all having the same generic name but a different species name, e.g. *Muntiacus muntjak, Muntiacus crinifrons*, etc.

In this scheme of relationships—the classification system—the Muntjac deer, together with the Tufted deer (*Elaphodus cephalophus*), are a separate group and are separated out as a sub-family, the Muntiacinae, which is one of the major divisions of the family Cervidae.

The scientific or Latin name of the animal can be difficult to get used to but it does have the great advantage that anywhere in the world that name uniquely identifies a particular animal; this is why the system has been developed and maintained by scientists ever since its formulation by the Swedish naturalist Carl Linnaeus in the eighteenth century. Indeed, the system of double naming—the binomial system—is often referred to as the Linnean system after its founder. For precision we must therefore use the binomial system but it is not the language of everyday speech. The forester does not say that a *Capreolus capreolus* has been eating his

Pinus sylvestris. Politely he will say that a Roe deer has been eating his Scots pines! Within a given country with a single language, the common names are generally well known and accepted. The problems arise first of all between different languages where each has a different word. The English Roe deer is in French *le Chevreuil,* in German *das Rehwild* and so on throughout Europe. In Asia the forest deer nearly all have different dialect names and in India the names 'Swamp deer' and 'Barasingha' can mean the same or different deer depending on which area you are in. In Europe the Elk is *Alces alces* but in North America it is called 'the Moose'. In America *Cervus canadensis,* a larger version of the European Red deer is known as 'the Elk' or 'the Wapiti', and so it goes on, confusion after confusion.

A lot of people have tried to standardise the common names but their work has lacked the authority that the Linnean system with its precise rules can apply to sort out the scientific names. Thus, we have the situation where there is almost total agreement on the scientific names of the deer (the rules allow for change in certain circumstances where new information necessitates amendment) but no certain agreement on the common names. The system that I am going to use throughout this book is something of an arbitrary choice. The list of scientific and common names to be used is derived from that given by Desmond Morris (1965) in his book *The Mammals, a Guide to the Living Species,* and that given by G. K. Whitehead (1972) in his book *Deer of the World.* The two lists are essentially similar, but there are differences in the species recognised which cannot be reconciled here.

A species is a distinct kind of animal. At first species were defined by a combination of external appearance and the size, shape and form of parts of the body structure. Taxonomists favoured the skull and teeth, size, and the colour and markings of the pelage for the definition of a species. This work was based largely on the study in Museums of the skins and skulls brought back by various expeditions, and took little account of other aspects such as biology and behaviour. New species were frequently founded on a very limited number of specimens and sub-species created for very minor variations.

The heyday of the mammalian taxonomists was in the nineteenth and early twentieth century when many new animals were being discovered as new areas were opened up for scientific study. Since this time a range of biological subjects from genetics and behaviour to reproductive physiology and biochemistry have become a vital part of taxonomic research. Species have also been more fully studied and collected in the field so that much more data is now available. As a result there has been a great deal of reassessment of the nomenclature and status of many species. In this reassessment, ideas about the deer have changed very little, but at a lower level ideas on the sub-species (varieties or races of a species) have been substantially revised. As a result, many names have been found to refer to the same animal (i.e. they are synonymous) and others are found not to have been valid at all. As a result of this revision we now have a much clearer picture of the composition of the deer family.

It was once thought that each species was a single act of divine creation and was therefore immutable for all time. Charles Darwin however showed that species were not immutable but were changing in response to the pressures applied to them. Thus evolution (change) through natural selection became a fundamental concept in taxonomic research. It thus became possible to think in terms of a species varying from place to place and with time. The generally adopted definition of a species was of a group of animals capable of interbreeding and producing fertile offspring. This practical test of a species cut right across the necrophilic basis of the anatomical delineation of species and has caused many problems in some animal groups. The deer however are in most cases sufficiently different from each other to cause little problem of definition.

An important feature of any population is its inherent variability and defining this is an important task in delineating both species and sub-species. Where the environment of a species varies greatly over its range this is frequently reflected within each species by variations over this range. Each population of a species will have certain features peculiar to itself even if they are not readily detectable. The White Tailed deer of the Americas is distributed across both the USA and Canada and as far south as Peru and northern Brazil. Over this range, there is a great deal

Fig. 2.1　Southern Pudu deer buck.

of variation in both size, biology and to some extent no doubt, in behaviour also. There is a general tendency for the members of the northern sub-species to be larger than those of the more southerly ones. There is however, little difference in colour and markings over the range, but as might be expected, the timing of those events in the annual cycle controlled by seasonal factors reflects local conditions.

The total population of a species can usually be subdivided into relatively discrete geographical regions, usually defined by physical features such as mountains, large rivers or a particular habitat type. Within these regions are many local populations, between which there are no fundamental barriers to inter-mixing.

Because of the physical barriers however, little interchange occurs across the regional boundary. Within this region the deer population has developed in isolation in relation to that environment and therefore differs in some measure from those of other regions. Where these differences are definable or where the region is sufficiently distinctive and discrete, the population may be defined as a race or sub-species. If isolated for long enough, this sub-species might well become a distinct species, but this takes a long time. The different sub-species are capable of interbreeding and producing fertile offspring, but do not do so for lack of contact. Sub-species are recognised in the Linnean system and are distinguished by the addition of a further (sub-specific) name after the scientific name. Thus there are thirty-eight recognised sub-species of the White Tailed deer *Odocoileus virginianus*. The sub-species found in the Florida Keys is distinguished as the Florida Key White Tailed deer *Odocoileus virginianus clavium* and the Yucatan White Tailed deer which ranges from Yucatan to Honduras as *Odocoileus virginianus yucatanensis*. Often given in parentheses after a scientific name is the name of one or more persons and a date. These are the names of the persons responsible for the first full description of the animal and the date of publication of the description. Thus, the Andean Guemal is fully described as *Hippocamelus bisulcus* (Molina, 1782) indicating that the first full description of this animal giving it that name was published in 1782 by Molina.

It follows that by creating discrete populations on say an island, that new varieties may well be created, and in time these might merit sub-specific status. Sub-species created by artificial means do not assist our understanding or delineation of the natural processes of evolution of our deer population. They belong more to range management farming and thus may have a significant future in that context.

The sub-species reflects the total interaction of the physical environment with the animal. Man has not been content with this and has frequently re-juggled the gene pool by the translocation of animals. In the USA there have been many movements of animals from one area to another for a variety of purposes. The same is true in Europe for the Red deer, Roe deer and Fallow deer.

Fig. 2.2 Female
White Tailed deer.

Most of these shifts are to 'improve' the quality of the deer which normally means that the landowner wants to produce bigger 'heads' of antlers to increase the trophy value of his population. Such introductions have frequently not been successful. Animals that have developed their characteristics in one environment (say, in a park in southern England) may not be suited to the new environment (say, a Scottish hillside). In such situations natural selection may very soon restore the *status quo*.

In other areas new introductions may be a restocking or an

entirely new introduction. In the British Isles the formerly ubi-
quitous Roe deer had almost become extinct by the eighteenth
century and many of the present populations stem from animals
brought from Europe. In Melbury Park in Dorset, in southern
England, is a long established herd of Red, Fallow and Sika deer.
It was recently noticed by Richard Prior that some of the adult
Red deer were spotted and he subsequently established that these
had come from a particular area of Hungary in the last century
where this unusual variety is still found.

A new environment can provide both opportunities and checks
for a species or sub-species. In New Zealand many deer have
become successfully established in the montane forests of the
South Island and the Red deer introduced from Britain exceed in
size of body and exuberance of antler growth any free-living Red
deer found in Britain today. The deer have flourished and with no
natural predator have severely damaged their habitat so that their
long term future will be very different from their short term
success.

A species threatened with extinction can usually be saved and,
relatively speaking, it may not be too difficult to finance and
implement a preservation programme. Often however it is more
difficult to protect a sub-species that is known locally rather than
internationally. Sub-species of natural origin are an integral
part of the species as a whole and of the wildlife of a region. Sub-
species have evolved over hundreds and thousands of years, so
that their loss cannot be made good by introductions from other
areas. Preservation and protection are both a local, national and
international problem. Had the animals been disappearing as a
result of the natural evolution of the regional ecosystem, then
they might perhaps have been allowed to go as part of the long
term evolution of the region. However the human race has
produced a modified ecosystem which it hopes will continue to
follow fundamental natural processes in an artificial situation.
In most cases all forms of endangered wildlife are threatened
by direct or indirect human actions rather than fundamental
shifts in the long term natural controls. For millennia *Homo sapiens*
was an unimportant, omnivorous fraction of the ecosystem.
Cultivation, domestication and technology have now established

Fig. 2.3   Herd of Manchurian Sika deer in summer coat.

mankind as the most important short term determinant of the future of our biosphere. With such power vested in us, we cannot permit the extinction of the variety of our wildlife and the protection of both species and sub-species of deer is a matter of urgency and responsibility. Some sub-species of deer have undoubtedly become extinct in recent years and others are at a critical stage.

The Sika deer of the Far East has 13 sub-species, many of which are in danger of extinction. The sub-species of Manchuria and Korea are not considered to be in danger but the three races in China are thought to be under very great pressure but precise information is lacking. The sub-species on Formosa is now thought to be extinct in the wild. Of the six races in Japan, only the small unspotted race of the Ryukyu Islands is in danger. In 1964 it was estimated that only about 30 individuals survived on the small (123 hectares, 304 acres) island of Yakabi.

In many areas, local races are undoubtedly threatened, although accurate information is lacking and conservation is impracticable in present circumstances. The worst of these areas are those parts of South-East Asia where wars have been raging for many years.

It is also possible to foresee problems arising in the future, notably in South America as development pushes its way into the forests and wooded grasslands. Conservation here is not a matter of rescue operations for threatened populations but of long term education and planning.

In Europe, the Red deer *Cervus elaphus* is well established, but three of its Eastern races, the Kashmir Red deer or Hangul *C.e. hanglu*, the related Shou (*C.e. wallichi*) of south-east Tibet and the Yarkand deer (*C.e. yarkandensis*) have declined drastically in recent years. Populations have never been vast, so that the response to increasing pressures has been correspondingly swift. In difficult terrain the collection of data is not at all easy and practical conservation is accordingly uncertain.

The Survival Service Commission of the International Union for the Conservation of Nature and Natural Resources (IUCN) is the organisation responsible for the operation of the threatened deer programme. Twenty-seven species and sub-species of deer are currently under threat of extinction over their world range. IUCN's programme for threatened deer aims to ensure their survival and to restore their productive status. In Chapter 3 IUCN ecologist Colin Holloway describes the state of the programme in an article which first appeared in *Deer* the journal of the British Deer Society. I am grateful to the society and to Dr. Holloway for permission to reprint this article with some updating as the following Chapter.

3 Threatened Deer of the World: Research and Conservation Projects under the IUCN Programme*

Introduction

In January 1974, the International Union for Conservation of Nature and Natural Resources launched a programme for the study and management of Cervidae that were considered to be threatened with extinction throughout their world range. Its objectives were, first, to ensure the survival of these species and sub-species and, secondly, to restore their productive status in the wild. The purpose of this article is to provide a summary review of research and conservation developments during the first twenty months of the programme.

During the period 1971–73, the programme was discussed and approved by IUCN's Survival Service Commission, which has international responsibility for conservation of all threatened species, and the membership and terms of reference of SSC's Deer Specialist Group, the Commission's advisory body on Cervids, were revised to take account of its new tasks and responsibilities under the programme. Governments, conservation organisations and interested individuals in countries in which threatened deer occurred were provided with details of the programme and invited to co-operate in its implementation. A field survey and a detailed deer study were undertaken and completed before the official launching of the programme, as pilot projects. This preparatory phase was completed by the publication of a description of the programme, which reviewed and analysed the conservation

* Contributed by Colin Holloway, Ecologist, IUCN, Switzerland and reprinted here with the kind permission of the author and original publisher.

Fig. 3.1   Threatened deer of the world, July 1975, showing geographical location: 1 *Moschus moschiferus moschiferus*; 2 *Muntiacus crinifrons*; 3 *Muntiacus feae*; 4 *Dama mesopotamica*; 5 *Axis kuhli*; 6 *Cervus duvauceli* (2 sub-species); 7 *Cervus eldi eldi*; 8 *Cervus eldi siamensis*; 9 *Cervus nippon taiouanus*; 10 *Cervus nippon keramae*; 11 *Cervus nippon mandarinus*; 12 *Cervus nippon grassianus*; 13 *Cervus nippon kopshi*; 14 *Cervus albirostris*; 15 *Cervus elaphus corsicanus*; 16 *Cervus elaphus wallichi*; 17 *Cervus elaphus barbarus*; 18 *Cervus elaphus hanglu*; 19 *Cervus elaphus yarkandensis*; 20 *Cervus elaphus bactrianus*; 21 *Cervus canadensis macneilli*; 22 *Odocoileus virginianus leucurus*; 23 *Odocoileus hemionus cerrosensis*; 24 *Hippocamelus bisulcus*; 25 *Hippocamelus antisensis*; 26 *Blastocerus dichotumus*; 27 *Ozotoceros besoarticus* (3 sub-species).

status of the threatened deer, provided a research framework for the collection of data to guide conservation practices, and invited participation of interested universities and research organisations (Cowan and Holloway, 1973, 1974).

The programme has included a variety of projects and initiatives, which, in practice, fall into two main categories. First, the collection of data on threatened deer (which range from status surveys of a few weeks to etho-ecological studies of two or three

Fig. 3.2   Male and female Hog deer in winter coat.

years duration). Secondly, the promotion of more effective management of species and their habitats, which normally comprise proposals based on results of the research projects. IUCN endeavours to maintain regular contact with the government concerned throughout the duration of the project and every effort is made to ensure continuing involvement and commitment of local government and private personnel.

Review of Current Studies and Conservation Developments

There are twenty-seven species and sub-species of Cervidae currently listed in the mammal volume of the Red Data Book as being under some threat of extinction throughout their world range (Goodwin and Holloway, 1972). Their names and approximate geographical locations are shown in Fig. 3.1.

The Calamian deer (*Axis calamianensis*) was actually added to the Red Book early in 1976. It is virtually restricted to Busuanga (900 sq km, 347 sq miles) and Culion Islands (400 sq km, 154 sq miles) in the Philippines and its total population is almost certainly less than 1,000 animals and continues to decline as a result of uncontrolled hunting (Grimwood, 1975). Other deer presently under review as candidates for inclusion are: the Burmese Brow Antlered deer (*Cervus eldi thamin*) from South East Asia, and the northern Pudu (*Pudu mephistophiles*) and Dwarf Brocket (*Mazama chunyi*) from north-western South America.

The greatest proportion of threatened deer taxa (approximately 70%) occur in Asia, followed by South America with approximately 15% of the total. In March/April 1974, the writer visited six countries in southern Asia (Burma, India, Iran, Nepal, Pakistan and Thailand) to examine the feasibility of initiating projects under the threatened deer programme. A similar exercise was undertaken for South America (Argentina, Bolivia, Brazil, Paraguay and Peru) by Dr. Hartmut Jungius, World Wildlife Fund (International) in April/May 1975.

The following notes cover only species or sub-species on which some recent development has occurred in regard to their study or conservation. The animals are treated in systematic order and background information on distribution and status is taken from the Red Data Book unless otherwise stated.

The Himalayan Musk deer (*Moschus moschiferus moschiferus*) occurs in high altitude woodland and dwarf scrub in the Himalayas, from Pakistan to eastern Tibet. It has been seriously depleted by uncontrolled exploitation for musk, a secretion produced in an abdominal gland of the male deer and used in the perfume industry and oriental medicine trade. In 1973, dried 'musk pods' were being sold for the equivalent of £300 each in India and Nepal, which effectively makes the Musk deer the most valuable deer in the world.

There is considerable interest in Musk deer farming, following Chinese success in extracting musk from the live animal and the subsequent proliferation of deer farms for musk production. A proposal to start a Musk deer farming project in Bhutan is presently under consideration by FAO. Trade in musk from wild deer has now been banned in most Himalayan musk producing countries and a number of reserves have been, or are in the process of being, established for the deer's protection. In late 1974, the Government of Himachal Pradesh established a new national park at Manali, in the Kulu Valley, of approximately 1,000 sq km (386 sq miles) which cover one of the principal Musk deer ranges in India. In 1977, IUCN hopes to publish a monograph, in English, to summarise Soviet experience in the study and management of the Siberian Musk deer (*Moschus sibiricus sibiricus*), and to initiate a detailed study of the Himalayan Musk deer, probably in the Langtang area of Nepal.

Fea's Muntjac (*Muntiacus feae*) has a very restricted area of occurrence in mountainous evergreen forests of southern Burma and West Thailand. There is no recent information on its status in Burma. Since April 1974 field surveys into the status and distribution of this Muntjac in Thailand have been made by a US Peace Corps biologist. Precise determination of the deer's distribution has been hampered by the occurrence of two other forms of Muntjac in the same region. The original range of Fea's Muntjac has apparently contracted, although it probably extends further south than was formerly believed. It is restricted to the immediate border region with Burma, where effective conservation measures are presently impracticable (C. R. Miller 1974/75, personal communication). Density and inaccessibility of the species' habitat coupled with the restriction of human movement in these border regions will undoubtedly provide a measure of protection for it in the foreseeable future.

Rediscovered

For several decades, the Persian Fallow deer (*Dama mesopotamica*) was considered to be extinct until its rediscovery in the mid-1950's in riparian forest along the Dez and Karkheh rivers in southern Iran. Sectors of these forests have been reserved principally for the conservation of the Fallow deer, but human pressure in these valleys is intense and the deer populations are still considered to be very low. A captive breeding group has been established in an enclosure of 55 hectares (12·4 acres) at Dasht-e-Naz to the north of Tehran and the herd numbered over 30 animals by early 1974 (E. Firouz 1974, personal communication). A study programme, financed and directed by the Department of the Environment and presently concentrated on the deer in the breeding enclosure, has been in operation since 1973. The study proposals are in the process of being expanded and the project has been included in the IUCN programme.

Kuhl's deer (*Axis kuhli*) is a rare species found only on Bawean Island (5,000 sq km), which is situated about 150 km (93 miles) north of Java. A recent report on the island and its wildlife describes the deer's preferred habitat as secondary forest and young teak (*Tectona grandis*) plantations. The animal's numbers are almost certainly declining as a result of hunting, using nets and dogs, and pit-traps. Population size is unknown but is thought to be not less than 500 deer. Proposals have been made to the Indonesian authorities to eliminate hunting (Kuhl's deer is totally protected by law), and IUCN and World Wildlife Fund have been requested to organise and fund a study of the deer under the threatened deer programme (Blower, 1975). A researcher for the project has been found and it is hoped to launch the study early in 1977.

The Swamp deer or Barasingha (*Cervus duvauceli*) occurs in deciduous woodland and moist grasslands in North and Central India and in Nepal. Following a decline over several decades, the population has started to increase within the past few years as a result of conservation measures and presently numbers around 5,000 animals. The northern race *C. d. duvauceli* comprises some 95% of this population figure, whilst numbers of the southern race *C. d. branderi*, although increasing, are still extremely low. Both sub-species have been the subjects of detailed studies in the threatened deer programme.

The study on the northern race began in February 1974 in Sukla Phanta Reserve, in South East Nepal, and is being conducted by a graduate research student from the University of Michigan. It covers investigation into deer population density and structure, daily and seasonal distribution and activity patterns, rutting and fawning behaviour, habitat utilisation and forage preferences, and study of interaction with human beings, including problems such as marauding (D. Schaaf 1974/75, personal communication). The main stronghold of the northern Swamp deer in India is Dudhwa National Park in Uttar Pradesh. It contains well over 1,000 Swamp deer and the Central Government provided (1974) a grant of Rs. 210,000 ($19,365) for the construction of staff quarters and provision of vehicles and equipment.

Research Project

The research project on the southern race of the Swamp deer was undertaken in April 1971–73, before the official inauguration of the threatened deer programme, by a graduate research student from the University of Zurich. It took place in Kanha National Park, Madhya Pradesh, which is the only area in which this sub-species of deer still occurs. The study identified the causes of the deer's decline and made proposals to rectify these situations; the researcher's thesis has now been published, in English (Martin, 1975). The recommendations, to reduce human disturbance, provide for year-round migrations of the deer and improve the structure and composition of grassland vegetation, have been very effectively implemented and deer numbers have increased from an all-time low of 60–70 in 1969 to about 200 in 1974 (H. S. Panwar 1974, personal communication). During the writer's visit to Kanha in December 1974, a Swamp deer was observed in the Halon Valley, outside the national park, for the first time in at least eight years.

The most endangered deer in the world is probably the Manipur Brow-Antlered deer or Sangai (*Cervus eldi eldi*). It is presently restricted to one sector of the Keibul Lamjao National Park (10·7 sq km, 4·13 sq miles), a swamp south of Logtak Lake in Manipur State, India. Its numbers have declined steadily as a result of illegal hunting and other forms of human pressure in its diminishing habitat. An aerial count of the remaining animals, in March 1975, after the vegetation had been burned and natural cover was minimal, revealed only 14 animals (Ranjitsinh, 1975). There are about 30 Sangai in Indian zoos. The State and Central Governments are now combining efforts to effect a rescue at the eleventh hour. The Botanical, Geological and Zoological Surveys of India have each begun scientific studies on the deer and its habitat. The Central Government has provided a grant of Rs. 640,000 to construct a ditch to exclude cattle from the sanctuary, to provide for equipment, staff housing, check-posts and a boundary road, and to extend the captive breeding enclosure at the sanctuary's edge. Two pairs of Sangai have been moved to the enclosure from Delhi Zoo. The sanctuary staff has been increased and it is to be hoped that all remaining forms of human disturbance will be eliminated from the reserve in the immediate future. The Keibul Lamjao has now been up-graded to a national park and there are proposals for the establishment of a second reserve on the Logtak river banks to which the Sangai could be re-introduced from captive herds (Ranjitsinh 1975 and 1974/75, personal communication).

The status of the other two sub-species of Brow Antlered deer also gives cause for concern. The Thailand Brow Antlered deer (*C. e. siamensis*) has been seriously depleted by uncontrolled hunting and habitat destruction, resulting from warfare and local insurrection in the Indo-chinese peninsula. Investigation in North East Thailand suggests that the deer's populations are now critically low, although some animals have been observed recently in the Khao Yii National Park (C. R. Miller 1975, personal communication). A 1974 Chinese publication on the Brow Antlered deer on Hainan Island states that the deer still occurs in parts of nine counties but herds are few and scattered and the total population is small (I. Orr 1975, personal communication). The Burmese Brow Antlered deer (*C. e. thamin*) is now a Red Data Book candidate. Its occurrence in swampy grassland areas in Central Burma has brought it into conflict with cultivators (S. Hla Aung, 1974, personal communication). It occurs in at least two of the fourteen Burmese wildlife reserves (although protection of some of these areas is poor) and there is a thriving herd of over 30 animals in Rangoon Zoo.

Extinct in the Wild?

In June/July 1973, a member of the SSC Deer Group from the University of Michigan undertook a survey of the larger mammals of Taiwan. His investigations suggest that the Formosan Sika (*Cervus nippon taiouanus*) is now extinct in the wild. It was widely distributed on coastal flats, along river courses and in lower foothill areas, but much of its habitat has been lost to agriculture and surviving animals were subjected to intensive hunting. Probably the last animal in the wild (a pregnant female) was killed in 1969. Sizeable numbers (several hundred) still occur in deer farms in Taiwan, where they are bred for meat and for antlers, which are used in the oriental medicine trade. An area has been identified which, if reserved and managed, could provide a suitable re-introduction area (McCullough, 1974).

Over the course of some years now, there has been speculation as to whether or not the Shou (*Cervus elaphus wallichi*) is still extant. It occurred in South East Tibet and neighbouring valleys of Bhutan. There are no captive specimens in existence. Early in 1975, IUCN was informed from a very reliable source that the Bhutanese Forest Service, using experienced and knowledgeable personnel, had made extensive searches for the Shou in its last known areas of occurrence in Bhutan, but absolutely no trace of the deer could be found. Recent inquiries in the People's Republic of China suggest that the Shou may have already disappeared from Tibet before the new Chinese Government could enforce protection (N. Myers 1975, personal communication). Several species of deer have been pronounced extinct in the past, only to be re-discovered several decades later, but the chances that a remnant group of Shou could still exist in some isolated corner of its former range must now be regarded as very remote.

Populations of the Kashmir Stag or Hangul (*Cervus elaphus hanglu*), which occurs only in the Vale of Kashmir, have declined drastically since the late 1940s, from thousands to a few hundred by 1970. Its stronghold has always been Dachigam Sanctuary (90 sq km, 35 sq miles) and, by early 1974, anti-poaching operations and reduction of illegal grazing and other forms of human disturbance had apparently halted the decline of deer numbers within the reserve. A census in the main valley of Lower Dachigam in February 1974 recorded 90 deer compared with 72 deer recorded in February 1970 (A. R. Wani 1974, personal communication). Later in 1974, however, the CWWSC Expedition to Kashmir reported continuing problems of stock grazing and other forms of human interference within the sanctuary. Infinitely more disturbing was the fact that the expedition could find little or no evidence of Hangul populations outside Dachigam—even in areas adjacent to the sanctuary there was, apparently, no recent evidence of deer (Anon, 1975). An IUCN/WWF sponsored study of the hangul, to be conducted by Dr. Fred Kurt with a counterpart from the University of Srinagar, began in August 1975 and will continue over the next two years.

An IUCN field survey of the Bactrian deer (*Cervus elaphus bactrianus*) was undertaken as a pilot project in March 1973. It suggested that habitat loss through human settlement, stock grazing and reed burning had virtually confined the deer to a narrow strip of riverain woodland along the international frontier with the USSR (Petocz, 1973). Losses to the total population have apparently been more than balanced by increases on the Soviet side of the frontier, however, where the total number of Bactrian deer is currently estimated at around 625 animals. The increases have resulted from protection of the deer and its habitat and particularly from re-introductions of deer into parts of their former range. Thus in the Ramit Reserve, a dozen deer released in 1960/61 had increased to 190 head by late 1974 (Bannikov, 1975). Two research workers are currently studying the deer and the project is now part of the IUCN programme.

South America

Considerable interest and activity in conservation of threatened species already exists in several countries in South America and the threatened deer programme in this region will be mainly concerned with finding funds and scientific personnel, where required, for deer species that need priority attention and with providing international co-ordination for national initiatives.

The Chilean and Peruvian Huemals (*Hippocamelus bisulcus* and *H. antisensis*) occur in alpine grasslands and adjacent forest fringes in the southern and northern sectors of the Andes, respectively. They have been depleted primarily by over-hunting. Following preliminary field studies, a U.S. Peace Corps biologist has recently begun a detailed ecological study of *H. bisulcus* in Chile. The study is part of the IUCN programme and is being supervised by the Universities of Washington and of Colorado State. In Argentina, the Government is presently conducting a national status survey of both Huemals; the Peruvian Government is to organise a national survey of *H. antisensis* in 1977 (Jungius, 1975).

The Marsh deer (*Blastocerus dichotomus*) inhabits flood plains, marshes and savannas over an area extending from southern Brazil to north-west Argentina and from the southern tip of Peru

Fig. 3.3 Southern Pudu deer buck.

to northern Uruguay. Its populations continue to decline from loss of habitat to agriculture and from over-exploitation; it is especially vulnerable to hunting and to competition with stock when its habitat is periodically flooded. In Argentina, a national status survey of the species is about to be launched, and a new reserve for its protection is being planned in the Province of Corrientes. In Brazil, a survey and a more detailed study of the Marsh deer is being planned in the Pantanal, which is the species' principal stronghold. A captive breeding group has been established in the Sao Paulo Zoo and is being used for behavioural and disease studies (Jungius, 1975). In March 1977, George Scholler of the New York Zoological Society began a three-year study on the Marsh deer and Jaguar in Brazil.

The Pampas deer (*Ozotoceros bezoarticus*) has a discontinuous distribution over the plains of central South America. Its numbers have been reduced primarily by over-hunting and competition with domestic stock. There is some doubt as to whether or not two sub-species of this deer, *O. b. bezoarticus* and *O. b. leucogaster* are threatened throughout their world range and their retention in the Red Data Book is under review. There is no doubt about the status of the third sub-species *O. b. celer*, however, which numbers only about 100 individuals in the wild and has been recognised for some time as the most endangered deer in South America. It occurs in only three localities of north-west Argentina. A captive herd has been established, although breeding success has been poor and, to date, it has probably constituted more of a drain on the wild populations from which these animals have been captured than a safeguard against extinction of the deer (Jungius, 1975). A cooperative project on the Pampas deer between the IUCN, WWF, CIC and provincial government was begun in 1976 and is principally concerned with conservation measures. The national CIC representative, J. P. Staudt, is co-ordinating the project, on which several Argentinian scientists based at La Plata and an overseas consultant, Dr. J. Jackson, are working.

Discussion and Comment

There are two main causes of extinction: first, overexploitation of the species' populations and, secondly, modification of the species' habitat. Practically all wild animals and plants suffer to some degree from habitat disturbance and many, particularly the larger animals and plants, commonly suffer, in addition, from over-use.

Deer in naturally fertile habitats have frequently been ousted by the agriculturalist and most species of deer have been under particular pressure from the hunter because of their readily acceptable meat, hides, antlers and other utilisable products and, for many species, their vulnerability to capture by virtue of their size, gregariousness, and accessibility during breeding and migration (Cowan and Holloway, 1973). Indeed, it says much for the resilience of the Cervids that, in spite of these pressures, only one species out of forty (Schomburgk's deer, *Cervus schomburgki* in Thailand) and two sub-species out of nearly two hundred (the American Wapiti *Cervus canadensis canadensis* and Merriam's Wapiti *C. c. merriami* in North America) have definitely been exterminated within the past few hundred years (Whitehead, 1972). At least two other sub-species of deer (the Queen Charlotte Island

Caribou (*Rangifer tarandus dawsoni*) and East Greenland Caribou (*R. t. eogroenlandicus*) have certainly become extinct during this period but, according to Banfield (1961), both Caribou were evolutionary senile taxa and their disappearance was probably not attributable to human interference.

Two major conservation measures have normally been employed to prevent species' extinction: first, legislative control on hunting the species throughout its range and, secondly, reservation and management of sample areas of the species' habitat, thereby protecting both the species and its environment. The approaches are perfectly sound in principle but, in practice, they have often done little more than slow down the rate of depletion. All the world threatened deer have legal protection in at least part of their range and the majority occur within one or more reserves but, with a few notable exceptions, there seemed little prospect until recently of removing any of them from the threatened lists in the foreseeable future—unless it was to transfer some to the list of extinctions.

The basic reason for failure of conventional approaches appeared to be inaction through ignorance or default. Nominal protection was provided but no active steps were taken to restore populations—either the causes of population decline were unknown, or the causes were known or partially known but no remedial measures were taken. The purpose of the IUCN threatened deer programme is to identify the causes of a species' decline, to propose practical and realistic remedial measures, and to follow the implementation of these measures through, in contact with the responsible authorities.

The habitats of most threatened species have been subjected to considerable modification, and rapid depletion of their populations may have altered age structures and sex ratios or affected their behaviour to the point where simple protection of the animal and its habitat is not sufficient to rehabilitate and restore populations. Land management techniques practised within the species' habitat might have little relevance to its needs, or, indeed, might actually be harmful. To date, only one detailed ecological study has been completed under the IUCN Programme, namely the Swamp deer project in Kanha National Park, but it provides

Fig. 3.4 Axis (Chital) deer stags.

an instructive case history. The research project and supporting investigation by park staff suggested that the major causes of population decline were: (a) degradation of grassland composition and structure through excessive burning and stock grazing, which led to replacement of perennial grasses by annuals and weeds and encouraged low grass that probably favoured the more versatile chital (*Axis axis*); (b) restriction of range and loss of grassland habitat to agriculture and settlement; (c) spasmodic poaching; and (d) during the late 1960's unnatural exposure of the depleted population to predation, by baiting tiger for tourist viewing in the deer's main activity area. Reorganisation of grassland management, the movement of a village that was situated in a traditional farming area, better poaching control, elimination of tiger baiting in the meadows, and the expansion of the reserved area to provide for year-round movement of deer without disturbance has trebled the southern Swamp deer population in five years (Martin, 1975; H. S. Panwar, 1974, personal communication).

Most threatened deer species occur in isolated, rural areas of developing countries, where wildlife poaching and pressure on wildlife habitat, to graze stock, cut grass or collect fuel, is frequently intense. Protection is often minimal because wildlife staff are few, untrained and probably uninformed, for example, of the detrimental effects of habitat degradation on the wildlife they are employed to protect. Initiation of a scientific study on seriously threatened species under these circumstances, when some form of emergency rescue operation would probably seem more appropriate, might appear absurd but, apart from the data collected for subsequent management purposes, experience has shown that conservation within a study area invariably improves considerably from the time that the researcher arrives.

The presence of an independent observer, who visits all parts of the study area, follows animals at all hours and inquires into all matters that affect the species' population, tends both to deter law-breakers and to prompt greater effort from field staff. Overseas researchers in the IUCN programme always have a local counterpart, if available, who acquires experience during the project and can continue research work when the principal leaves. Researchers commonly provide some ad hoc training for field staff and their progress reports to IUCN/WWF ensure that the status of the threatened species is kept under international surveillance and early warning is provided of impending crises.

In the foreseeable future, the main requirements of the threatened deer programme are a continuing source of funds and of research workers with suitable academic qualifications and the temperament to be able to work in isolated areas, often under difficult conditions. The majority of funding for the programme, to date, has been provided by the World Wildlife Fund. No project has yet been delayed or discarded through lack of funds, but WWF has a great many calls on its resources and sooner or later some additional funding sources must be tapped if the present momentum is to be maintained or increased. Continuing financial support depends on achievement. It is too early to try to judge the effectiveness of the programme on the number of threatened deer taxa that have been saved. The programme's main achievement to date has been in generating an enormous amount of interest, enthusiasm and activity in threatened deer. There has probably been more activity in the study and management of world threatened deer during the past two or three years than in the whole of the past twenty-five years since organised international involvement in threatened species began.

4 Form and Function

If we look at four very different kinds of deer, we see at a glance that in general build, proportion, etc. they are essentially similar and it is likely that most people would name them as deer rather than as, say, carnivores. The similarity in general structure between such widely distributed species suggests that they have an essentially similar way of life; this is so. Deer are adapted to life in the wood and scrubland and only a few, such as Reindeer and Scottish Red deer, now have races which have evolved for life in more open landscapes.

Deer are of slender graceful proportions. The elongated body is supported by four long slender legs and terminates in a short tail. At the opposite end, the neat angular head is set on a slender neck of moderate length. The ears are set high on the head, well back. They vary in size and outline but in general are ovoid or triangular and well developed. Forward of the ears and also located high and well to the side are the eyes, which are large and round. Above the eyes in the male are the two columnar bony outgrowths of the frontal bone—the pedicles—on which the antlers are developed. The nostrils are located at the tip of the nose above the narrow mouth. Associated with them is the area of black skin, the rhinarium, which is extensively self-patterned.

The body markings vary between the species and also seasonally. The body is almost entirely hair-covered and may be either of plain colour or marked by a pattern of pale spots on a dark ground. These markings are confined to the back and flanks which are always darker than the underside of the body and neck and which, except for a throat mark in some species, is always unspotted.

A specialised pattern of markings is associated with the tail and perianal region. Basically, the pale skin of the anal area is highlighted by surrounding pale hairs often bordered by a darker

Fig. 4.1 Adult Fallow deer in summer coat with well grown antlers in velvet.

fringe. When alarmed, these hairs are erected to display prominently this white flash, which is a very effective visual signal over a considerable distance, as many a deerwatcher knows to his cost. The fact that so often it is a vanishing white rump that the observer sees, is also a testimony to the effectiveness of the body markings as camouflage. Too often, of necessity, we look at deer in zoos or parks and wonder whether the orange brown coat of the Roe deer or the dappled coat of an Axis deer is not in fact too conspicuous. Seen in the natural habitat, however, the effectiveness of the pattern and colour (plus the body shape and behaviour of the deer) is well demonstrated, especially as its natural enemies probably see it almost entirely in monochrome.

In some species distinct tufts of hair or skin markings reveal the site of scent glands. The Sika deer and also the Roe deer and White Tailed deer have prominent tufts of hair on the outer side

37

Fig. 4.2   Adult Roe deer buck in winter coat showing the movement of the ears, the rump patch and the glands on the metatarsal bone.

Fig. 4.3   Adult Reeves Muntjac, showing the frontal and pre-orbital glands.

of the metatarsal bone just below the ankle joint. These hairs are associated with the location of cells producing a specific secretion. The two parallel hairless areas about 3 cm (1¼ in) long on the forehead of a Muntjac deer are considered to be secretory glands though I have never seen or smelt any secretion from these although the forehead area is rubbed on small saplings and strong stems of shrubs and grasses. In contrast, the large deep pit found just in front of the eye in both Pere David's and Muntjac deer is lined by skin and is actively engaged in secreting a strong smelling, soft, buff-coloured waxy substance.

Not all skin glands are so readily visible, the forehead gland of the Roe deer, for example, is very diffuse and the secretory cells do not form a visible feature. Elsewhere on the body are found other secretory glands about whose activity and use little is known at present.

Deer are graceful animals especially when moving. A variety of gaits (Dagg, 1973) and speeds are to be seen together with leaping and bounding movements. The hooves are cloven and the surface area of the foot in most temperate species is small. It is somewhat larger in Pere David's and Reindeer that have evolved to cope more effectively with snow cover and boggy ground. The bounding ability and powers of jumping are a function of the elongated limbs, but more especially arises from the relatively greater length and powerful musculature of the hind leg. It is this that provides the propulsive force. Movements in deer have not been well studied. My own impression is that they vary with the situation, ranging from a walk, slow trot, to a gallop as necessary. However, at some point in a fast movement they may begin to leap and bound and I am not sure whether this is produced as a response to a particular stimulus or at a certain speed. This phenomenon is not confined to deer, but is also found in many antelopes. This bounding during fast movement is not to clear an actual obstacle but is part of a behaviour pattern the function of which is not understood. The leap which covers quite a lot of ground, may serve to increase the effective speed of the deer. The movement may also distract or confuse a following predator and it certainly leaves fewer scent points on the ground, making a trail harder to follow in undergrowth.

Play by both adults and young has its own repertoire of movements. Chasing play is a regular part of the early life of the fawns, notably in the young of social species such as Red, Fallow, Sika and also between siblings in species such as Roe, Chinese Water deer and White Tailed deer. These may also join up with other young encountered on favoured feeding areas. The young display amazing agility, twisting and turning, side stepping and bucking at great speed. It is not often appreciated that adult deer may also indulge in play, usually in the form of chasing. It is rarely seen either in the wild or captivity, but on several occasions I have seen Fallow bucks, does and fawns, up to ten animals, playing chase. This appears to have no connection with play that is part of a learning process of social behaviour, but seems rather to be a *joie de vivre* situation.

Play is part of the process of learning and growing up and there seems to be an almost universal invitation to play, common at least to a great many species. This is the stiff-legged bounce often accompanied by a bobbing and weaving of the head and neck as a display in front of the desired playmate. Commonly, a youngster will come bouncing up to another, display and then dart off sideways inviting a game of chase or if the other responds by moving off, chase is given. Chase is not over any great distance but consists of twists and turns in which the role of chaser and chased is exchanged in a moment. The stiff-legged bounce is frequently seen in frisking young and adults as well.

Deer jump with precision at speed. When catching them, I have seen a Chinese Water deer approach a suspended long net of 9–10 cm ($3\frac{1}{2}$–4 in) mesh at full speed and without check, detect and dive through an 18 cm (7 in) hole, barely twitching the net. Deer often seem to choose to go under or through an obstacle rather than jump it. When forced to they will, however, clear a very substantial obstacle such as a solid wall. I have seen a pregnant female Muntjac, from a standing start, jump clean over a brick wall 2·4 m (8 ft) high. Of the larger deer, I have little of my own observations to go on. I know of a Red deer stag that during the rut came and went as he pleased to a group of hinds enclosed by a 2·4 m (8 ft) iron fence and he presumably went over it. Similar feats are known for other such stags and also Fallow deer. However, both of these species are normally retained by somewhat lower fences.

Externally, the deer also resemble their close relations the antelopes and cattle, all of which are built to live as swift-moving plant eaters in the temperate and sub-tropical landscape. Basically, they are built as mammals, having the same basic digestive, glandular, skeletal and nervous structures as most others. It is in the detail of the structures that the specialisations appear and these relate mostly to feeding.

Feeding begins with the mouth, and in particular with the teeth. There are two kinds of teeth in the mouth that are important—the four pairs of incisors in the front of the lower jaw—the cutting teeth—and the three molars and three premolars on each side of both the upper and lower jaw, 24 in all, known also as the cheek teeth. These are for grinding up the food. The front teeth are vitally important, for it is these eight that actually cut the food—grass, leaves, etc. These eight lower teeth bite against the gum of the upper jaw and not against teeth as in man, dogs and horses. Loss of front teeth can occur due to mechanical damage, infection of the gum, fluorosis or wear in extreme age and usually leads directly or indirectly to death, as the animal is unable to gather sufficient food, especially in the winter months. Except in the case of extreme age and physical injury, it is unusual to find many animals in a population with severely affected incisors. It does, however, occur in areas where pastures are exposed to airborne pollution from industrial processes, notably fluorine poisoning from brickwork discharges. In such areas, teeth are soft and abnormal patterns and amounts of wear are the rule rather than the exception.

Ingested food is not chewed to any extent and is normally swallowed and stored in a special compartment of the stomach, the rumen/reticulum. From here it is regurgitated as a bolus and this cud is then chewed and swallowed again, this time into a separate compartment (the omasum) and thence into the fourth chamber (the abomasum). Cudding is done at leisure in a secure place. The cheek teeth are built and arranged as shredders and grinders to break up the tough plant fibres so that the digestive juices and micro-organisms can work effectively on the plant substance. Cheek teeth work as two occluding sets, the upper and lower teeth on each side working as a pair together. The cheek teeth are made up of folds of enamel, cement and dentine which produces an abrasive surface of tough, sharp ridges and furrows. It is these opposing surfaces working with an elliptical jaw movement that shred the plants. These are very powerful grinders working with the full power of the large masseter muscles that control the vertical movement of the jaw. A finger caught by a jaw stroke will be heavily bruised and lacerated. Chewing the cud is a lengthy process as each bolus takes about fifty strokes before it is swallowed.

There is occasionally present in the upper jaw a small canine tooth. This may be present in almost any species. In some, such as Red deer, it is normally present. In others, such as Roe, it is only occasionally present. In these deer it is largely a functionless remnant, a relic from their great ancestors who had large canine teeth for fighting. These large canines are however present in both Muntjac and Chinese Water deer which resemble some of the first deer. These long, sharp tusks are capable of inflicting severe wounds. The deer themselves probably suffer less from their use than do predators such as dogs or foxes.

From the mouth the food passes via a long muscular tube (the oesophagus) to the stomach. The stomach of most ruminants is similar between species and its four chambers represent a specialised development to cope with the problem of gathering and processing large quantities of plant food in relative safety. Deer 'eat their fill' several times a day and probably spend about three times as long cudding it as they do gathering it. From the stomach,

Fig. 4.4   Adult male Chinese Water deer, showing the large canine tooth.

the food passes successively through the small and large intestines, in which the nutrients and water are absorbed into the body. Towards the end of the large intestine the contents become drier and begin to form the distinctive pellet shaped faeces.

The uterus of the female is located in the rear portion of the abdomen and is connected by the vagina to the external opening situated immediately below the anal opening beneath the tail. Both openings are normally covered by the tail. The uterus has two distinct chambers which are continuous with each other. The two halves are known as horns. From the top of the horns the narrow fallopian tube leads on each side to an ovary. The ovaries vary in size with the species. They are frequently bean shaped, about 3 cm (1¼ in) long in Pere David's and about 1 cm in the smaller species. With age they become misshapen. The eggs are shed from the ovaries, fertilised in the fallopian tubes and develop in the uterine horn. The uterus contains a number of

Fig. 4.5   Non-pregnant uterus of the Roe deer.

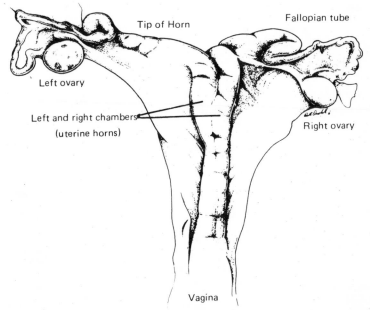

Fallopian tube

Fallopian tube

Tip of Horn

Left ovary

Left and right chambers
(uterine horns)

Right ovary

Vagina

special structures—the caruncles are round or elongated ridges which with the developing embryo will form the placenta— the structure which enables the mother to nourish and maintain the developing young. In most species a single young will be found in either the right or left horn with equal frequency. Twins are almost invariably found as one in each horn. Multiple births fit in as best they can. In the Reeves Muntjac, and apparently also in Pere David's deer, the left horn of the uterus is barely developed compared to the right and the young must always develop in the right hand side.

The testes of the male are located in a bag-like fold of skin— the scrotum—between the hind legs. The penis is located in front of this and is normally retracted. Sperm is conveyed to the penis from the testes by a pair of tubes, one on each side—the *vasa deferentia*—and on the way other secretory glands also discharge into the tubes to produce the seminal fluid in which the sperms live. The penis is also the organ by which urine is excreted. In deer, urine is also used to convey chemical messages so that there may be other secretory glands located so as to discharge into the urinary ducts. During the rut, urination is associated with scent marking and the excretory function is largely incidental.

The young are suckled by the mother from the four teats of the mammary gland, which is located between the hind legs. All species have four teats irrespective of the number of young and all four are capable of functioning, though how many are maintained in full use during a lactation is uncertain.

Control of the various cycles within the body is regulated by a number of glands which have a feedback relationship with the master glands. These peripheral glands include the testes and ovaries, the adrenals, thyroids, parathyroids, etc. The overall regulation of the reproductive and several other cycles is by the pituitary gland located at the base of the brain and it is this that regulates those cycles which are related to the external environment. Compared with their importance and effect, these glands are small. Even in a large Red deer the pituitary gland is only about 1–2 cm ($\frac{1}{4}$–$\frac{3}{4}$ in) long. This is possible because of the potency of the hormones which they produce.

5 *The Four Senses*

Deer perceive their environment through the senses of vision, hearing, smell and touch, exactly the same senses as are possessed by man and other mammals. The eyes, ears, nose and tactile organs are receptors and, when stimulated, they send coded signals as nerve pulses to the central nervous system and brain. The brain interprets these signals and appropriate action is initiated. It is the brain that interprets the signals and thus the experiences that are stored in the memory determine how an animal will react to a particular stimulus.

As human beings we know that our reaction to a stimulus may be different from that of another person. Some odours are liked by one person and disliked by another. The taste of a substance may be different between two people and the identical substance may taste different to the same person on different occasions. Testing how we and other species perceive is extremely difficult and has to be done one item at a time, whereas in the real situation our senses are subject to a continuous barrage of stimuli. Most of these do not even register in our consciousness—they are part of a general background that we do not knowingly evaluate. Because of these complexities in perception and evaluation, we cannot experience or describe the environment as the deer experiences it. We can only look at the sensory organs themselves, the way we see them used and how the deer react.

There is no doubt that the deer builds up in its brain a normal spectrum of sights, sounds and smells for a particular environment and it is differences from this and warning signals within it that alert the animals.

Deer rapidly become accustomed to heavy road, rail and air traffic, grazing within a few yards of a road edge because passing traffic does them no harm. A car which stops to watch may also be tolerated but a door opening will usually put them to flight. Deer also become accustomed to regular work in a forest and come to ignore the noise and scents of power saws, tractors and bonfires. A trail through a woodland nature reserve passes within 15 m (39 ft) of an area frequented by deer and people walking the path do not disturb them. Stop and observe them closely and they become agitated and may even move off.

Deer have good but not exceptional eyesight. When feeding on open ground their vision is very much restricted by surrounding vegetation. The sense of smell is also restricted when feeding by the immediate aroma and the fact that airborne scents do not normally travel close to the ground but above. The first line sense then is hearing. Feeding deer will rely on sound for the first warning of danger. A sound that is part of the normal spectrum of background is ignored, but a breaking twig, a sharp or discordant sound, will bring them to full alert and the whole battery of senses will be brought into play. An alerted deer will bring its head and neck up, the head directed to the source of the sound, the ears erect and forward focussed towards the spot, the moist nose twitching sampling the air and the eyes trained for any sign of movement. Detection is now a matter of luck. My own impression of the visual acuity of deer is that, whilst they readily detect any sign of movement their powers of resolution of detail are not very good. On several occasions I have escaped detection out in the open by freezing even though I was a discordant object in the landscape. On the other hand, there are perhaps some species whose discrimination is much better.

Visual detection is undoubtedly aided by sound. Watching the movements of the ears co-ordinated with the eyes leaves little doubt that the ears are functioning as directional aerials and can be used to pinpoint a sound. Normally, a search is accomplished using both eyes and ears so that the chances of detection are much increased. Some support for the view that it is sounds and smells rather than the visual environment that are the dominant experience comes from observation of the effects of wind on deer behaviour and this also applies to many other ungulates. Strong winds are associated with turbulent air conditions, a constant mixing of air streams with no regular direction and a high level of

1   Red deer stag.

2   Young male and female Chinese Water deer in first winter.

3   Young male Chinese Water deer in first winter.

4 Reindeer bull on the island of Spitzbergen.

5 Sika stags in Woburn Park, England.

6   Female Rusa in the early spring.

7   Head of young Rusa male.

8 Adult male Hog deer.

9 Two Pere David's deer stags in the early spring. Note the velvet being cleaned from the antlers, and the moulting of the dull winter coat revealing the glossy red summer coat beneath.

10 Pere David's deer. Adult stag, hind and calf in summer coat.

11 Pere David's deer with antlers in velvet during the winter.

12   Swamp deer stags in the Kanha National Park, India.

13   Adult Fallow deer bucks in early autumn, showing almost fully grown
      antlers in velvet and some of the colour varieties found in this species.

14 In agricultural areas, Fallow deer often lie up in cereal crops in the summer months—just like this buck.

15 Fallow deer fawn approximately six hours old, concealed in bracken.

Fig. 5.1   An alert female Japanese Sika deer in summer pelage.

background noises which replace the normal spectrum. By virtue of these noises being of infrequent occurrence and of a varied nature, they are unfamiliar. One may hazard a guess that the senses are almost blocked in regard to normal operation in much the same way as sunspot activity affects radio transmission. Deer in these conditions appear bewildered and panicky and in captivity injuries often result on these occasions.

Clear reception of sound is essential for precision listening. Air currents and the vibrations they produce in and around the ear tend to blur the sound, and therefore a form of damper is very desirable. This appears to be achieved in many species by the hairs in and around the ear. Sometimes horses are clipped in the

47

winter, but hair inside the ears should never be removed. If accidentally done, the horse's behaviour leaves no doubt that its sense are upset and it becomes very agitated. The dense hair found in and around the ears in many deer probably acts as a damper improving the quality of sound reception in turbulent air. They also act as insulation. In some, but not all, tropical species, however, the ears are only sparsely hair-covered.

The sense of smell is a vital part of the early warning system. Deer's noses are very sensitive to smells, chemical scents forming a part of their normal language of communication. Human beings also have individual smells, but except in extreme cases we do not consciously respond to them. These aromas are however readily detected by other animals. Scents are carried on the air and most movement of air occurs several inches above ground level. Most scents are carried in the air streams at about the same levels as they were released at. In the wild, however, terrain and vegetational cover create turbulence and the direction and speed of the air varies. Within these limitations the deer can use scents on the wind as a warning of the presence of other animals and alert the other senses accordingly.

So far, sight, hearing and smell have been considered as detectors of potential enemies—a rather limited function. In practice, all senses are combined but each has its individual cues. The eyes, for example, are used for the recognition of individual animals of the species and for other forms of visual assessment, varying from size and strength to the viability of the newborn. They are used to find and select food, and to see what is happening and where the animal is going. The eyes are perhaps not so important as one imagines for I have known of several blind wild Fallow deer that ran with the herd and appeared relatively unaffected by their condition.

The ears are used for listening, not just to the background but also to the individuals of the herd. If one can approach close enough to Red or Fallow deer, and no doubt to many others as well, one can hear a more or less constant 'conversation' going on. This is quiet and low and consists of whispers, grunts, bleats, etc., made apparently by all the group. This sort of communication presumably reinforces the identity of the group. It has, how-

Fig. 5.2   Female North American Mule deer in winter coat.

ever, not been studied or recorded as far as I am aware and indeed the whole question of sound communication in deer awaits study.

Just as speech is the most complex communication system consciously used by man, communication by scent is probably the most elaborate used by deer. A scent is the perceived effect of a chemical on our noses. Most of the scents used as chemical messengers are very complex molecules and little is known of their nature in the mammals. We can define two groups of scents: those produced by other organisms, which are merely recognised as such; those produced by the species for internal communication, i.e. they are species-specific. Species-specific scents, as we understand them at present, are mostly related to sexual condition or status definition. There are characteristic scents associated with

49

the various stages of the oestrous cycle in the female and these are ascertained by the male. Males also apply scents from a variety of glands to trees, bushes, the ground, etc. and it is thought that these both characterise the holder and define the area of a territory. There is no doubt that, despite our ignorance of and insensitivity to the olfactory environment, to the deer it is a major language.

The fourth sense, that of touch, is one that we tend to overlook in deer, for unlike ourselves, they do not have any appendage obviously associated with touch like our own hands. In fact, the part of the body most involved in contact between individuals is the muzzle, mouth and tongue. In the mother/young relationship, nuzzling and licking is extremely important for the wellbeing of the young and reciprocally for maternal satisfaction. One can often see a fawn becoming bored with its mother's enthusiastic licking. In the adult there seems to be little physical contact between the members of groups of Red, Fallow and Pere David which I have observed. Two of our Chinese Water deer, however, spent a great deal of time nuzzling one another. This lack of contact in the adult contrasts with, for example, horses—but is paralleled in the field behaviour of sheep and cattle. I have excluded fighting behaviour from this category, but to some degree there is an adaptation to this in that the antlers, the appendages most used in combat, are devoid of nerves.

There is one last sense whose character is very poorly understood. This is the sense associated with the vibrissae (whiskers) of the face. These are strong, long bristles each of which terminates in an innervated pit arranged so as to detect any movement of the whisker. It is thought that in some animals the whiskers are concerned with the sensing of low frequency sound—the ears cope with the higher frequencies. This would account for their great development in aquatic mammals, such as seals and otters, and also moles. Their development varies between the species of deer—they are, for example, well developed in Red and Pere David's deer, less so in the Roe. They do not form a single detector area but are characteristically dispersed about the head in discrete groups. They are present in Red deer around the chin and muzzle with a further cluster of darker hue, one on each side, about 7 cm (3 in) back from the lower lip on the underside of the chin. A more diffuse cluster of dark hairs are found above and below each eye. In the Red deer these bristles are 5–7·5 cm (2–3 in) in length. In contrast, in the Roe deer they are finer, shorter and white in colour and appear to be confined to the muzzle and lower tip of the jaw—at least as far as gross appearance is concerned.

The distribution of the vibrissae in the Red deer suggests another possible function, that of protecting the eyes. Vision in the deer is very directional, and when feeding amongst scrub and bushes, they would not be able to judge the distance of twigs and branches outside of the very limited field of forward binocular vision, which is extremely narrow in close up situations. The vibrissae are located in what would appear to be blind spots. As sensor organs projecting beyond the body they would provide tactile warning of the proximity of twigs, etc. to the eyes and muzzle. Injuries to the head attributable to branches, etc. are very rare and this might be due to the effectiveness of the vibrissae in this respect.

Fig. 5.3   Adult female Pere David's deer in winter coat showing the small hairy ears and the facial vibrissae.

6 The Social Scene

Observations of the groupings and dispersions of deer are frequently reported in largely anthropomorphic terms and this is so widespread in the literature that some cautions are necessary. Deer are polygamous animals and the idea of a family of mother, father and young as a social unit is not known to exist in any species of deer. The nearest approach to this will be seen in species such as the Roe, where females with young may be largely resident within the territory of a single buck or, as in Muntjac, where a male keeps company with a female with a young fawn. It is possible that some of the young will be the offspring of the older animals. Whilst deer do recognise individuals, it is not known whether they recognise their offspring once grown or after a period of separation. Despite the objections to the use of the term 'family', it is a convenient and not necessarily misleading term to apply to small groups of females with young at foot and yearlings in attendance.

The term 'herd' is variously used to describe larger associations of deer than the family, though no formal limits are set. Here, the term herd is used for the total population of deer in a discrete area that largely act in common. It is essentially a management term, generally more convenient than precise except where there are substantial physical barriers restricting the movement of the animals. The term 'cohort' will be used for individual groups of any size that are found within the herd from time to time.

At least for the scientists, the myths of deer associations, movements, etc. were exploded with the advent of studies using individually marked animals and radio tracking techniques. Most of this new work began in the 1960s and much now in hand is concerned with studying the problems identified in the pioneer studies and also applying the results to actual management situations.

The amount of information available is therefore rather limited and in this section I shall concentrate on describing some of the factors involved in studies of social groupings and dispersions so that the reader can apply these to more individual situations, and will use only a few studies of species to indicate the problems involved.

In a given area the dispersion of the deer at any time will be related to:

1   Available food
2   Disturbance
3   Climate
4   Social behaviour (Staines, 1974).

The first three are external factors and apply year round. The fourth is intrinsic and its significance can vary through the year. Fallow deer, for example, are grossly intolerant of other males only when they are herding females during the brief autumn breeding season. Interactions at other times of year are much less severe.

There are two terms—'home range' and 'territory'—that are used to describe the area utilised by an animal. Behaviourists are not agreed on the finer points of definition of these terms, but essentially home range refers to the area of ground used by an animal to meet its physiological and psychological needs in the course of its life. This lifetime home range may be quite extensive, much more than in any one year and we shall examine why this may vary from year to year. The size will also vary greatly between sedentary and migratory species and the nature of home range between these two groups is rather different. Territory is the area of ground which an animal will define and defend against others. Some animals have year round territories, others defend territories only at certain times of year and in others territory is a matter of distance about an animal. Territories are usually thought of in an entirely male context defended by males against males—and as areas that others are kept from. I am not sure that these ideas are entirely appropriate for all deer. Are females entirely passive in terms of the ground they occupy or are there forms of territorial behaviour in the females of at least some species (e.g. the Roe)? How many species do not have a defended territory

Fig. 6.1(a) The territories of
Roe deer bucks in Cheddington
Wood, Dorset in 1967.
(Redrawn from Bramley, 1970.)

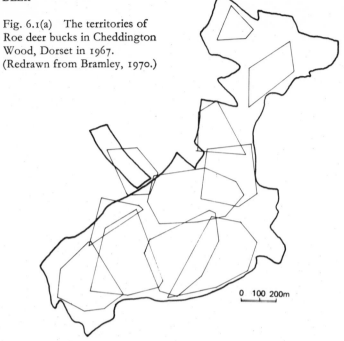

0 100 200m

Fig. 6.1(b) Aerial photograph of Cheddington Wood.

at all? A lot more study is required before these questions can be satisfactorily answered.

The general characteristics of territoriality and range in the Roe deer have been established by Paul Bramley (1970) working in Cheddington Wood in Dorset, England. Bramley found that the 113 hectare (279 acres) woodland contained eleven territorial males (see Fig. 6.1) and this number remained constant for the three years of the study. In the final year, the total population of 61 comprised 11 territorial bucks, 12 non-territorial bucks, 21 adult females and 12 male and 5 female yearlings (i.e. fawns). The territories were actively defended in the period April to August although there was some territorial behaviour prior to this. For the rest of the year all the sightings of these territorial bucks were within their territories. (It is by no means certain, however, that these animals do not come and go.) The bucks without territories would appear to have been mostly younger animals and these clearly led a difficult time during the spring and summer, being chivied and harassed by territorial bucks. The home ranges of these non-territorial bucks were larger than those of either territorial bucks or does and frequently traversed the territories of several bucks. The majority of these non-territorial bucks were not seen in the wood in the following year, so that a territorial system would appear to promote the dispersal of young males. Whilst territorial bucks were intolerant of the younger ones, there was little aggression between the holders of adjacent territories except in March when these were being reestablished. Also, there were few changes of ownership of territories over the three years.

The home ranges of the Roe deer does at Cheddington overlapped each other considerably. In some cases, from one to three does ranged largely within the territory of a single buck, whilst others ranged across the territories of two or three bucks.

The Roe were usually to be seen in small groups and the maximum size of group seen by Bramley was eight. In the first five months of the year, the biggest groups were seen in February and March. Over this time exactly 50% of the groups seen comprised three animals, 31% comprised four and the remaining 19% varied from five to eight. It is interesting to see how the composition of these groups changed from the non-territorial phase of January

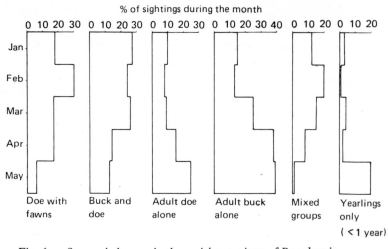

Fig. 6.2 Seasonal changes in the social groupings of Roe deer in Cheddington Wood, Dorset. (Drawn from data given by Bramley, 1970.)

and February into the territorial phases of April and May. There are six significant groupings:

1. Doe with fawns of previous year (i.e. 6–9 months) at foot;
2. Adult buck and doe without young;
3. Adult doe only;
4. Adult buck only;
5. 'Winter group' bucks, does and fawns of previous year;
6. Yearlings only.

From Fig. 6.2 it will be seen that in January and February the most frequent associations seen are does with their young of the previous year, a buck and a doe and mixed age and sex groups. In March and April the bucks and does without young appear to separate, and in April solitary adult bucks and solitary does form 38% and 15%, respectively, of the sightings. In May, the month in which the does mostly give birth and when the adult males are actively territorial, one sees the break up of the association of a doe and her fawns of the last year and a corresponding increase in the numbers of young bucks and solitary young does.

It is interesting that territorialism takes place during the breeding season, and serves to disperse younger males from the area, and does not occur in winter when any food shortage is actually experienced. Presumably, non-territorial behaviour in winter ensures that the whole population can have access to the food of an area. In such feeding situations, however, there will no doubt be some kind of pecking order but I do not know what this is or how it acts. The bucks are in velvet during the winter.

The home range of an individual Roe will depend on his status in the population and this is why, for a real understanding and effective management, the term home range must be redefined. We may use either the lifetime home range or the home range in a given year. For practical purposes, a theoretical model of how the home range changes with age and environment can be deduced into which actual data can be put. For the first 11 months of its life, the Roe fawn is strongly bound to its mother. It will therefore occupy the same home range as the mother and probably also her social status. Increased agonistic behaviour shortly before birth drives away the previous year's young so that these yearlings must now find their own place. The female will mate as a yearling and appears to be acceptable within the population as a whole. We do not know of any intensive agonistic behaviour that would disperse the young doe nor, however, is there much positive indication of what did happen to them at Cheddington. At Kalø in Denmark, however, the indications are that the yearling females that do disperse do so because of the change in the mother/young relationship (Strandgaard, 1972).

The yearling buck is antlered and will be fertile and is a potential competitor for a territory. However, his chances are slight in a well populated area. Thus, in the second year, the buck must live as best he can between the territories or emigrate. The second year and third year are likely to be spent searching for a territory, and wintering wherever conditions are favourable. In the fourth year it is likely that a territory will be found or fought for. There is, however, nothing to stop this happening earlier. Once a territory is established it appears to be held for several years and the buck then becomes relatively sedentary. Subsequent displacement may result in further movement or the acceptance of non-territorial status.

Many species of deer are observed to live in larger groups than the Roe and these include the Fallow (Chaplin and White, 1970) Red (Darling, 1937) and Sika (Horwood and Masters, 1970) and probably many others of the genus *Cervus*. The Fallow, Red and Sika are all temperate species and the general principles determining their social organisation are likely to be similar. The Red and Fallow deer are the most studied of the three and offer certain advantages for study in that the Red deer are found in both woodland, hill and park settings and the Fallow in both woodland and parkland.

The general strategy of social organisation can be deduced from the numerous studies of Red deer in these habitats, and can be illustrated by reference to the studies on the island of Rhum by Lincoln, Youngson and Short (1970). For ten months of the year the population is split up into stag and hind groups. The range of stag and hind groups is different during this time. Different groups of the same sex have a distinct range but there are areas of common ground. Stag groups vary in size but usually comprise less than 20 individuals. The members of stag groups are sexually mature and range from the older animals down to the new recruits who are usually 3–4 years old; Fig. 6.3 shows the composition of two of these groups in 1969. Within these groups there is a strong dominance hierarchy.

The hind groups vary in size and comprise not only the females, but also the yearling and calf stags. Stag groups would appear to be fairly stable at least as far as mature animals are concerned. There is some movement of 3–4 year old stags between groups until these settle and establish their place in the hierarchy. The groups over-winter on the lower ground ranging over about 202 hectares (500 acres). During the summer the groups range much further and take in hill ground covering about 810 hectares (2,000 acres). In late September the feeding groups break up and the stags wander considerable distances to find hind groups. Rutting stags attempt to herd and defend a group of hinds against contenders and it is the older stags who first take over followed by younger stags. Many of the older stags return to areas where they have rutted in previous years and these rutting areas are mostly established in places which are feeding grounds common to several hind groups. The rutting area is usually outside of the

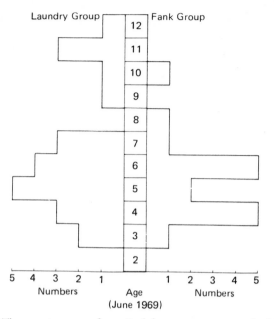

Fig. 6.3   The age structure of two Red deer stag groups on the island of Rhum in January 1969. (Drawn from data given by Lincoln, Youngson and Short, 1970.)

normal home range of the stag group, and may be a considerable distance away. No area of ground is defined as territory by the stag. Instead, the territory is a mobile one, a matter of distance around the hind group. Yearling stags in velvet at this time that would normally live with the hinds are not tolerated and must await the end of the rut to rejoin the females. Once an individual's rut is over, it returns to the home range of the stag group and these gradually reform during October and November.

In different areas of Scotland, the size of groups and the extent of the range vary because of the different intensities of influencing factors at different locations, and the state of the population. In woodland, where it is much more difficult to study these questions, group size is generally much smaller. This, as much as anything, may be due to the generally smaller populations and smaller area of effective habitat available. However, anyone who has studied deer in woodland will appreciate that the few situations in which the deer are readily seen may well not be typical of the normal structure. In deer parks the picture is essentially the same. There are separate groups of stags and hinds and except during the rut, these do not intermingle to any great extent unless forced to do so by disturbance or incorrect artificial feeding techniques. These groups have their preferred areas according to the weather and time of day.

The Fallow deer also has a similar organisation (Chaplin and White, 1970) with relatively minor differences in detail. Except during the rutting season in October and November, Fallow deer populations comprise groups of adult males and separate groups of females and young. The separation of yearling males from the female group occurs during autumn and winter and is perhaps triggered by the sexual maturity of the yearling buck. Some yearling males will keep loose company with the female group over the winter, others join male groups, but most are not yet firmly attached and often wander seeking a group to join or an area in which to settle. This applied to the park populations and also to the woodland areas surrounding these parks where I was able to observe them fairly readily. Observations of wilder woodland populations are not precise enough to determine what is actually occurring. In the wild and also in parks, the buck groups are generally smaller than the female groups during the winter and numbers vary greatly. In the wild, I have seen regularly during the winter doe groups of 30–70 animals and these would appear to be the bulk of the population in that area. It would seem that there is a tendency for Fallow to congregate in much larger numbers than the Red deer. This trend can also be seen in park herds, especially where the two are mixed. At any time of year the bucks seem much warier than the does and are difficult to locate, let alone assess clearly. What has, however, been noted by many observers in the wild, and also in parks, is that the bucks and does occupy quite distinct areas of the country which contains the herd as a whole. Thus, some woods are almost exclusively buck areas and others are occupied by the does. My impression of the Fallow deer in the mosaic woodland/agricultural landscapes of southern England is that the does as a herd move around a comparatively large area in response to local pressures. This area may be as much as 25–50 sq

Fig. 6.4 Japanese Sika deer stag herding hinds during the autumn rut.
All the deer are in winter coat.

km (10–20 sq miles) in big populations or under 13 sq km (5 sq
miles) in the case of smaller herds of, say, 30–40 animals. These
figures are estimates from my own observations and discussions
with other observers and should be taken as a guide only. At rutting there is a considerable movement of animals and the traditional rutting areas taken up appear to be largely in the normal
range of the does. Much more work needs to be done on this
species.

More difficult than most to study are the small Asian Muntjac
deer. My own and other observations of the Reeves Muntjac
living wild in Britain have established a number of features of the
social organisation of this species (Chaplin, 1971, 1972; Dansie,
1970). Most of my observations were made between September

and May in woodland as outside of this time the vegetation is too thick for effective simple observation. Most of the sightings were of single animals, bucks or does feeding and foraging. Within quite small areas (about 4 hectares or 10 acres) one could be fairly certain of locating an animal. In time, when some of these were individually recognisable, the same animal was to be found in the vicinity, particularly where food from pheasant feeding was available. However, very few individuals could be recognised and this pattern perhaps reflects a fairly even dispersion rather than small fixed ranges.

Does were rarely seen with young at foot, probably because of the rapid development of the fawn (weaned at 7–8 weeks) and the fact that the fawn lies apart from its mother and even in captivity does not often follow. Usually, when there was a fawn present, a buck would be in company with the female, perhaps because of the post partum oestrous found in this species. Obviously, pregnant females were not seen in company with males. The largest group of Muntjac seen did not exceed five; these two groups were seen regularly in two separate areas feeding beneath Yew trees ap-

Fig. 6.5 Fallow deer, buck and doe on rutting stand.

parently searching in the ground litter for red berries. These were seen in January and February and the group comprised an adult buck and doe, a young doe and a fawn. Occasionally, another female would be present. These were regularly seen for several weeks and appeared to be resident in the area. Over several years the natural congregation of animals on to favoured feeding areas in late winter was not seen. This occurred with the Chinese Water deer in the same wood but not with the Muntjac. The nearest approach to 'herding' of this species was due to the activities of the pheasant keepers who acted as a feeding centre for animals living in the surrounding areas. In the absence of marked individuals, I have drawn no firm conclusions from the many sightings of these deer in the Woburn woodlands in England. I suspect that in these woodlands they are essentially solitary animals, coming together for mating. They would seem to survive in quite a small area, perhaps about 2–4 hectares (5–10 acres) maximum, and such an area might well contain several animals. Essentially though, this species remains an enigma.

Aspects of social organisation in the Reeves Muntjac and of

Fig. 6.6 Reeves Muntjac foraging in an English woodland.

behaviour in both the Reeves and the Indian were studied in France by Dubost (1970, 1971) using zoo park animals. The study of the social organisation of the Reeves is of interest but because the structure of the population was atypical, the conclusions that can be drawn are rather limited. The study of the behaviour and of the interactions of both species is however most valuable in establishing the repertoire of behaviour used by these animals in the social and sexual context. A conclusion from the study of the territory of the Reeves was that the females established and actively or passively defended a small territory against other mature females. The boundary of the territory was marked by scent and piles of dung. The male in contrast roamed across a much larger area covering the territory of several females. In the Woburn study area which covered several hundred acres of woodland and contained about 200 Muntjac, there was no evidence of territories being established or marked and defended by either sex. If anything, the indications were rather to the contrary, the animals appeared to have a home range and were not intolerant of the presence of others. In a large breeding group of Muntjac, maintained in captivity for many years and with a constant input and output from the group, a well marked dominance order was established, but there was little aggression between the members despite the very small size of the enclosure.

In the Red deer groups, patterns of social behaviour and relationships are firmly established. The stag groups have a well marked dominance hierarchy which regulates behaviour and relationships. This dominance hierarchy is an important biological regulator in the population. Each individual animal must find for itself a place within a stag group at an early age. At first this is a subordinate position. So much so that the young stag may try and join another group. Once in, the animal may either actively or passively try to improve his ranking. It is a feature of the system that once established an older stag will not often change his group.

In each stag group, each animal knows its place and dominance can therefore be asserted by slight gestures rather than threat displays. Normally, dominance can be asserted by a look or flick of the head or merely by the approach of a dominant animal. For this reason the observer is rarely made aware of the strength of the system. Overt aggression occurs only when a subordinate does not react to the warnings of a dominant one, and this is usually an indication of an impending physical contest to determine whether the rank order should change.

Rank is established by intimidation and/or physical contest and a major factor in success is size, weight and fitness. It follows that mature animals in their prime are likely to be dominant to both

Table 6.1 Dominance Order and its Relationship to Age, Antler Characteristics and Recruitment in the 'Laundry' Group of Red Deer Stags on the island of Rhum in January 1969*

Name	Age (years) (June 1969)	Antler size (no. of points)	
		1967–68	1968–69
Laundry group			
Crusader	11	13	15
Devil	12	10	10
Aristotle	11	9	11
Broken Brow	9	8	9
Caesar	10	9	9
Ravel	7	8	9
Manfred	11	8	11
Friction	6	9	11†
Tricky	6	10†	12
Oscar	7	10†	12†
Ringo	6	6†	7
Fancy	6	8	10
Cecil	5	8†	10
Tim	5	6†	8
Buddy	5	7	8
Friendly	5	6†	9†
Nelson	5	8	8
Symmetry (castrate)	7	8	velvet 4
Recruits in 1968–69			
Midge	4	—	8
Inward	4	—	8
Mite	4	—	7
Droopy	3	—	8
Pointless	3	—	6

* From Lincoln, Youngson and Short, 1970.
† Antler broken in hard horn.

the younger and also the more elderly ones. Growth and development occur over as much as 5–6 years in stags so that the highest ranked stags are likely to be in the 7–12 age range. Table 6.1 shows the age and rank order of two stag groups on the Scottish island of Rhum. A stag attaining a high rank has proved his ability to survive in that environment. The higher ranking stags are the first to rut so that these animals will fertilise the majority of the females. Females in good body condition come into oestrous earlier than those in poorer condition. Condition is also a measure of survival ability so that natural selection operates by mating the fittest with the fittest and thereafter the less proven with the less fit.

This selection is exercised at the population level as well, for whilst in the area, group dominance regulates daily life; rutting does not take place within the area group structure. Rather, there is a dispersal of stags to more distant areas where each stag must assert himself against all comers. Distances travelled are considerable and there is thus a mixing of genes and a wider testing of the stag's fitness.

The social organisation of the Reindeer presents some interesting contrasts for in this species the population is to be found in mixed sex herds for nearly all of the year. Within these herds there is a strong pattern of social dominance involving all members of the herd, in which the ranking changes through the year (Espmark, 1964).

The Reindeer is found over a vast area of the circumpolar region in Asia, Europe and Canada, so regional variations in at least some aspects of social organisation and behaviour are to be expected. Broadly speaking though, Reindeer are found in herds of mixed sexes and ages; often these herds are subdivided into groups of a few to several hundred animals (Thomson, 1971). At other times they are in much greater numbers, often in their thousands. The really large aggregations occur at times of common purpose, such as migration. There is, however, no restricted local home range or distinct male and female areas. Rutting occurs in the autumn, once antlers have hardened in both sexes, and in the build up to this there is a great deal of sparring and fighting to establish rank orders. During the rut males tend groups of females and are kept

Fig. 6.8   North American White Tailed deer, buck and doe in winter coat.

thought to be sedentary. Of ten female yearlings known to have emigrated six were killed, an average of 6·8 km (4·2 miles) away (range 2·9–10·1 km; 1·8–6·3 miles). By comparison, the study suggested that adult does, i.e. two years or more, did not leave the home area in any significant number. A few males, however, moved away as adults.

Yearling does normally regrouped with their mother and her fawns during October, but where the yearling also had fawns the regroupings were later, largely in December. In succeeding years nearly a half of these family groups broke up in the following June and the former yearlings did not rejoin their mother in the next winter and of those that did reform, most broke up the following summer. In this study it was found that eight appeared to be the maximum number of animals that would bed together and regularly associate, and there were never more than three females of yearling age or older.

There are no major associations of adult White Tailed bucks or of mixed sex groups, except by chance on common feeding areas. Bucks are mostly solitary from early September to the end of January, but in February to the end of August, buck associations are normal. However, these are not large and of these social groups around 80% contained from two to four individuals. Bucks associate with the females only during the breeding season from October to January.

Thus in the female White Tailed deer the social grouping is very much a matriarchal/sibling affair. This family grouping suggests that adjoining groups of females are to a substantial degree related to each other in the female line. The males on the other hand, once mature, have a non-familial relationship with other bucks and a high degree of dispersion. Thus it is the male which ensures the genetic variety of the population.

7 Food and Feeding

For a given species of deer occupying a particular habitat there is a range of foodstuffs available. The availability, palatability and nutritional value of particular foods will vary throughout the year and over the centuries deer have adapted themselves to the pattern of food availability. The recent introduction of commercial forests in both temperate and tropical latitudes has however removed many of the food plants of the deer, so that the variety and year round availability of food may no longer be assured. As a result of this, there may be greater pressure on certain species, a switch to species not formerly eaten in any quantity, and seasonal crises of food availability or shortage of essential nutrients and constituents. These crises may well result in severe damage to the commercial species of the plantations as the only food source available. This is not a gourmet choice but a matter of starvation or malnutrition.

It is food quality and availability above all else that has brought the deer into conflict with commercial forestry and it is a situation of the foresters' own making. We can either continue with the policies of the past and try and wipe out the deer in our plantations, or we can pursue a constructive policy of managing the forests with deer as an integral part of the forest ecosystem. The former policy was an abysmal failure and made the situation worse. The integral policy has now been a largely successful exercise and the deer provide a considerable part of the financial return from recreational use of the forest and commercial cropping.

Whatever the habitat, deer numbers must be regulated to the year round carrying capacity of the habitat. The winter population is crucial for this is the time of the greatest food shortage. When wolves, bears, lynx and other predators filled our temperate forests we had a self-regulating system. Now we have lost this and the only natural controls left are food availability and disease. Anyone who has seen deer starving to death cannot fail to accept the fact that on humanitarian as well as practical grounds mankind must now take on the role of predator and regulate numbers in relation to the food supply. If we wish to live the way we do, if we wish to read books and to have the use of other wood-based products, then we must accept that numbers must also be compatible with an acceptable level of timber production.

In tropical areas there are similar conflicts. In more advanced countries, it is the deer versus agriculture/silviculture. In less developed areas, it is the conflict between the expansion of peasant cultivation with a rising population affecting habitat, predator and prey.

Food and feeding, despite their commercial importance, have not been widely studied in many species. This is, in part, due to the very complex and time-consuming procedures that must be used in order to determine what a deer has been eating, and the difficulty of deriving a valid generalisation of a year round food spectrum for different habitats. Our information can come from four different techniques. Visual observation of deer can be used to see which obvious plants are being eaten. Observations of feeding areas and of cropped plants in the sward can be helpful. More precise information is obtained by identifying the fragments of plants passed in the faeces or from the examination of the stomach contents of dead deer. In captivity, feeding trials may be used to determine food preferences and may also be combined with other experimental techniques for data on digestibility, etc. None of these techniques enables us to determine the precise diet of the wild animals and the nutritional benefit obtained. Such precision can come only from laboratory feeding trials. We are here concerned with the year round diet of wild deer in their environment so that the data collected in studies using these techniques are an approximation to this.

It is therefore not surprising that most of our information on the food of wild deer is largely empirical. Field observations and laboratory and field analysis can, however, combine to give us a broad view of the food spectrum of deer and their seasonal pre-

Fig. 7.1 Roe deer buck
grazing.

ferences within this. When backed up by analysis of the nutritional
content of the plants, it is often possible to see very good reasons
for seasonal preferences. These methods together give us a useful
background for predicting the likely food strategy of a species in
a given habitat. Where this indicates the likelihood of an in-
adequacy of supply or a seasonal deficiency, appropriate action
can be taken either by culling or by improving quantity or quality.
This is often a very simple procedure of fertilising a grass ride or
encouraging herb growth, or introducing or encouraging species
such as holly, which as a broad leaved evergreen is an important
winter food.

Because of these problems of diet, food identification and the
fact that most species have not been studied in this way, this
chapter will deal in generalities except where positive information
about a species is available that can be used to illustrate a point.

In the tropical and subtropical regions of the world there is
not the marked annual season change in the climate that there is
in higher latitudes. In some areas, however, there are dry and wet
seasons associated with the monsoon rains. We should, therefore,

73

Fig. 7.2   A clearing in deciduous woodland. The growth of forbs and grasses on these areas makes them very attractive to the deer for feeding.

view almost all deer habitats as showing some degree of variation through the year. It is to this variation that the flora and fauna have become adapted. In the temperate regions of the world, plant cycles are essentially seasonal and there is a period of dormancy for most native plants over the winter. The temperate seasonal climate, therefore, gives rise to periods of abundant foliage and times of scarcity. Plant growth depends on temperature and moisture, so that in areas that are moist and warm all the year round, plant growth occurs throughout the year with individual trees and plants following their own calendar. Where seasonal drought occurs, the different plant species each respond in their own way. The grasses may wither and frequently catch fire, but below the ground their rhizomes survive to send up new growth when the rains come.

The deer must select from what is available in each habitat. Looked at overall, the deer utilise essentially similar kinds of food. In wood and scrubland they browse on the bushes eating leaves, shoots and buds within reach, and on the ground they feed from the low growing herbs and grasses known collectively as forbs. In due season they will eat also fungi and fruits. In less wooded areas and grasslands they take a relatively greater proportion of ground plants. It is almost impossible to quantify the relative intake of grasses and herbs compared to browse, still less the nutritional contribution of each. However, my examinations of stomach contents of Fallow deer from deciduous woodland suggests that the bulk of this is from ground-growing plants that have been grazed. This is also true of the stomach contents I have analysed of Muntjac, Chinese Water deer, Red and Roe from deciduous woodland. All of these have from time to time also illustrated the opportunistic nature of the feeding in due season, e.g. beech mast and yew berries in Muntjac, kale in Chinese Water deer, crab apples in Fallow deer, etc.—but all are additions to a basic gut content of ground-grazed grasses and herbs.

Where specialisation of habitat occurs, this will be reflected in the diet. The Moose of North America feed extensively at certain times of the year on aquatic plants for which they will dive quite deeply. The South American Marsh deer will also have a feeding spectrum that reflects their habitat. Reindeer feed extensively on lichens and depend on them for winter survival. Summer brings a wider variety of ground herbs and scrub.

The chemical composition—to the deer, the food value—of a plant varies with different parts of the plant and through the year. Most of these changes reflect the need of the plant to provide for renewed growth and ensure its survival. Buds and growing shoots have a higher protein content initially than they do later in the season, when growth ceases and the leaves are functioning. Palatability may also change and it is now well established that the presence of chemicals at certain times is a protection against insect attack. Such substances may also render them less palatable to deer.

In the temperate regions, the deciduous trees and plants are essentially dormant and lacking foliage during the winter. With the approach of spring, activity begins and buds and leaves begin to form, shoots emerge and so on. Late spring and summer are a period of abundance with the rapid growth of plant tissue well able to cope with the predation of browsing and grazing animals. In autumn, the abundance is over and dormancy sets in. For the winter there are only the remains of the grasses and herbs, providing bulk but little nutrition and the occasional flush of grass. The only green plants are the evergreens and the leaves of holly and ivy and withered leaves of bramble.

Against this background of the vegetational cycle we have that of the deer evolved to cope with this cycle in each habitat. Feeding of the young may cease before the onset of winter, or if continued over winter it is at a very low level of production. Inside the mother is the foetus, usually entering its second trimester in the New Year. As spring comes the foetus begins to fill out and preparation begins for the birth in early summer. The male casts his antlers shortly before and both male and female enter early summer with intense physiological activity. Mating follows in the autumn and the cycle is complete. Thus, plant and animal are well synchronised, but as we look closer at some of the mechanisms involved, we see just how fine is the balance between the two and how swift and hard are the consequences of disruption.

In summer male and female are feeding intensively and their appetite is practically insatiable. This provides the wide spectrum of substances needed for the growth of the antlers and the production of milk to feed the young. Any food surplus to bodily maintenance and function is stored as fat. By the end of the summer the energy surplus is over and we enter the transition period when surplus gradually turns into the winter period of potential energy deficit. What this means is that in the normal course of events, a deer may not be able to gather sufficient food to meet its maintenance requirements. This is because what is available is of low nutritional content and there is not a great deal about. An animal driven by hunger may well find, on average, less food energy than it expends looking. It is for this reason that with the coming of autumn there is a voluntary drop in food intake, the insatiable appetite and heavy feeding characteristic of summer stops abruptly. This has been confirmed by experiments on White Tailed deer in the USA and we first noticed this in our work on rearing Chinese Water deer in captivity. As a result of this knowledge from captive animals, it was possible to suggest that this was also the case in Red, Fallow, Sika and Pere David's deer observed under more natural conditions.

This energy conservation works by cutting down the appetite. In Chinese Water deer, it followed the first cold nights and frosts. In terms of volume of foliage, the reduction was of the order of a half to one third the summer intake. Summer appetite was enormous, for no matter how much (within reason) hedgerow food

Fig. 7.3 A young female Reeves Muntjac cudding. Deer normally return to cover after feeding to chew the cud.

and grazing was provided, it was all consumed and this was not checked by the amount of fat clearly being laid down. Reducing the amount of food to a level still well above high plane maintenance only made the deer restless and when not cudding or eating they would be foraging. It was, therefore, no small personal relief to discover the fact of appetite reduction! Once reduced appetite became established, surplus food was not eaten.

Appetite reduction serves to conserve energy in several ways. It firstly cuts down the amount of time and movement involved in foraging and the time the animal is fully exposed to the weather. Wind and rain draw heat from the body at a rate proportional to their severity and the body surface area exposed to them. A deer laying up in cover is sheltered from wind and rain and the body area exposed is much less than when standing in the open. The difference between energy intake and expenditure through winter is normally a deficit, and this deficit is made up by the reserves of energy stored as fat. The normal biology of the animal requires this reserve of fat to be used up during winter. In zoos, therefore, there is always a danger of obesity when rations are kept at the same level the year round. In a good winter, the reserve may not be fully required for maintenance of mother and foetus, and the foetus may then receive additional nutrition and be larger and heavier than usual.

In spring, appetite is reactivated to coincide with the spring flush of plant growth. This highly nutritious feed is required to finish the developing foetus and to provide for the milk production necessary to feed it. These events are ahead of birth by 1–2 months depending on species. Reactivation is, however, a difficult time. Appetite is stimulated at the time of a spell of fine warm weather—at the end of March, beginning of April, in the south of England. At this point the deer are at their lowest ebb, often with little or no reserve left, depending on the severity of the weather. If this spell of weather is a false spring, i.e. it is followed by a return to winter conditions, then the deer are in trouble. Appetite demands that they search for almost non-existent food and energy is burnt up very rapidly and they soon begin to die of starvation. It is the winter/spring transition that is the time of heaviest mortality.

Deer move about in search of food. This may be a seasonal migration or a local movement. The areas of their annual range utilised on any one day will reflect the food available in the area, weather conditions and also any disturbance. Daily feeding movements are usually quite limited in terms of distance travelled. During the day, most feeding will occur in cover, but at night it is frequently extended to more open areas and cultivated fields. Species such as Fallow and Roe are thought to find most of their food within a broad range utilised by the animals and this range is usually definable and stable for most of the year. Food from the woodland and from adjacent fields is normally sufficient to maintain them in the area.

The more marked the seasonal difference in the climate, the less likely it is that deer can remain on the same ground year round. Annual movements of the herds occur between summer and winter grounds in both hill and mountain areas and also in the Tundra. In summer, the Red deer of the Scottish hills inhabit the hill tops, but their winter survival has depended on the availability of lower grazing and shelter areas mostly in the valley woodlands. It is, however, the valley bottom lands and lower hill zones that have been the most valuable ground for agriculture and forestry. In consequence, the deer have been deprived of land and food essential for their survival. In a good winter they have survived at the expense of body condition and fawn survival. At other times they have died. On occasions freak snowfalls or storm damage have broken down the protecting fences and the deer have entered the plantations and caused severe damage. In deer management, adequate provision must be made for winter feed and shelter. The commercial benefits of Red deer to an estate are now more fully appreciated and they are often artificially fed on the lower ground during the winter.

In Scandinavia, the Reindeer herdsmen move their animals from the higher summer areas to lower or coastal feeding grounds, a pattern probably derived from the natural migrations of their ancestors.

In the polar areas of Canada and Russia, the Tundra provides rich summer grazing for several million Reindeer. In winter it is, however, a cold foodless desert devoid of cover and incapable of supporting the large grazing herds. In order to survive the winter, the Reindeer have for centuries migrated southwards into the northern woodlands of willow and birch and coniferous species. Here, despite a greater snow cover, they find sufficient food and shelter for the majority to survive.

The necessity for both long and short distance migrations between winter and summer feeding grounds has resulted in the establishment of regular patterns of movement on the ground. This has been accompanied by the development of responses to environmental stimuli which indicate the onset of winter. The existence of these traditional migration routes has recently become a matter of considerable public concern in relation to the construction of oil pipelines across the Tundra. It is feared that these pipelines might drastically interfere with the migrations.

The digestive system of deer differs from our own in being based on a symbiotic relationship with bacteria and protozoa inhabiting the digestive tract. Their activity is concentrated in the first two compartments of the stomach, the rumen and reticulum. The digestive enzymes of the body are not able to break down cellulose, which is the major constituent of plant cells, and it is thus unable to use the glucose molecules of which cellulose is formed. The enzymes produced by the bacteria can, however, do this.

In the rumen (McDonald, Edwards and Greenhalgh, 1971) the carbohydrates—starches, plant sugars and cellulose are converted into organic acids such as acetic acid, propionic acid, etc. The acids—known collectively as the volatile fatty acids—are absorbed directly from the chamber and are subsequently utilised within the body. Proteins are also broken down in the rumen into simpler molecules, such as the amino-acids and some of these are further broken down into organic acids and ammonia. The ammonia is absorbed directly and conveyed to the liver and converted into urea. Some of the ammonia, and also other nitrogenous material, is synthesised by the bacteria into protein. The latter organisms are subsequently conveyed into the abomasum where they are killed, digested and subsequently absorbed in the gut. Thus, there are many complicated pathways of break-down and synthesis of the main bulk foodstuffs.

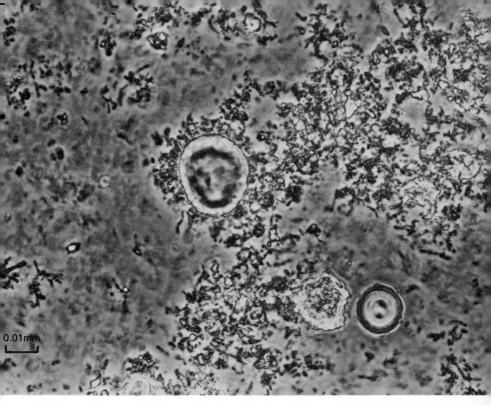

0.01mm

Fig. 7.4 Rumen sample from a Red deer showing in the centre a starch granule surrounded by bacteria.

There are something like ten thousand million bacteria in every square centimetre of rumen fluid plus several hundred thousand of the much larger single-celled protozoa. To maintain an efficient and effective rumen there must be a balanced intake of carbohydrate (cellulose) and nitrogen. The balance of these substances changes through the year and in winter in particular, not only is the cellulose difficult to digest because of the increased lignin content of plants, but the protein content is also low. For this reason the efficiency of digestion by the animal fluctuates through the year and also with the diet. To illustrate this point I have selected a detailed study of the diet and its digestibility through the year in the American White Tailed deer in Eastern Texas carried out by Dr. Henry Short (1971). However, before looking at this there are some interesting points of difference in the activity and character of the rumen between different species of deer

Table 7.1   Absolute and Relative Size and Capacity of the Rumen/Reticulum (R/R) in Deer and Domestic Livestock*

Species	Adult body weight (kg)	R/R volume as percentage of body weight	Weight of R/R contents of body weight	Weight of R/R dry matter as percentage of body weight
Roe deer	14	8	7	1·7
White Tailed deer	39	10	8	1·4
Fallow deer	40	14	9–12	1·6
Mule deer	57	10·3	7·4	1·07
Red deer	95	23	10–14.9	1·5
Sheep	45	25	13	0·64–1·15
Cow	450	26·4	14·1	0·96–1·88

* Data from Prins and Geelen, 1971.

which have not been appreciated in the past and should be looked at in many other species. The work was carried out by Prins and Geelen (1971) in the Veterinary Biochemistry Laboratory in Utrecht, Netherlands, and was done on Red, Roe and Fallow deer and sheep and cattle.

Small animals have a greater basal metabolic rate per unit of body weight than do larger animals. In Table 7.1 it can be seen that both indices of volume and weight of the stomach compared to size indicate considerable differences not only between domestic animals and deer, but also between the different species. Characteristics of the fermentation products suggest that there might well be differences in metabolic rate and food turnover between the deer. The digestion of cellulose is a rather slow process and it is, therefore, likely to be more efficient in animals with large rumens and greater retention times. It is interesting that the cellulolytic activity of rumen fluid declined from 9 in Red deer to 5·8 in Fallow and 4·4 in Roe deer whereas the index of amylolytic activity increased from 5·2 in Red deer to 6·1 in Fallow and 6·9 in Roe. In cattle it is about 3·6.

Seven species of protozoa were found in the rumen of Red deer, three in Fallow and only one in the Roe. In all three deer it was *Entodinium* that comprised all or most of those present

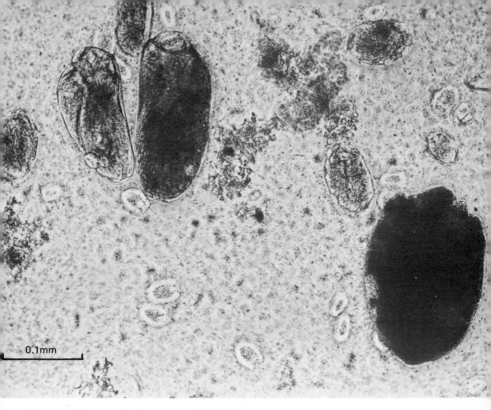

Fig. 7.5   Protozoa in the rumen of a Red deer.

followed by *Eudiplodinium* and *Diplodinium* in both Red and Fallow and also *Epidinium* in the Red. These species differences are thought to relate to the different rates of passage and the food characteristics of the deer.

The seasonal variation in the diet of White Tailed deer in Short's study is shown diagrammatically in Fig. 7.6. It will be seen that browse is the only major year round component, forming from 19–42% of the identifiable food. Forbs are only of major importance in May and grass is not an important item at any time. In July, mushrooms are a major constituent and in the autumn and winter acorns are of special significance and in February a large amount of pine is taken. The exact proportions of these items are to some extent affected by the difficulty of identifying different plant materials in the stomach. The diet itself is a product of that particular range situation.

The nutritional content of the different foods taken by the deer

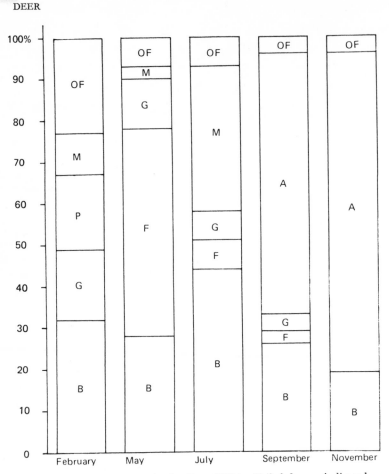

Fig. 7.6 Seasonal changes in the diet of White Tailed deer as indicated by the analysis of stomach contents. Minor components are not specified and the values are expressed as a percentage of the total dry matter identified. (Drawn from data given by Short, 1971.)
B = Browse F = Forbs G = Grass P = Pine A = Acorns M = Mushrooms OF = Other fruits and minor constituents

through the year was analysed and their degree of digestibility was measured *in vitro* in the laboratory (Table 7.2). There is little change through the year in the digestibility of the mixed browse and the pine but some variation is seen in that of the forbs which are mature and fibrous in November but more succulent at other times. On average the year round digestibility of the different components is very similar, varying between 25% and 30%, only that of forbs at 40% is significantly higher. These values indicate an average digestibility for mixed foodstuffs of about 34%, whereas a carefully formulated laboratory ration had a digestibility of 68% in these deer.

Tame deer were used by Healy (1971) to assess the forage preferences of White Tailed deer in a 7·9 hectare (17-acre) area that had been clear cut four years before to regenerate northern hardwood species in the Allegheny National Forest in north-western Pennsylvania, USA. A very different environment from that of Short's study. The time that the deer spent eating each kind of food plant was recorded and this was compared with the frequency and amount of growth of each food plant. The study highlighted the problem of quantifying food preferences and also of establishing the significance of the contribution of each plant species to the total nutritional pattern. What is shown very well, however, is the seasonal shift in emphasis from different categories of plant and the way in which the deer selected what they would eat:

'The deer were always selective when feeding. They sniffed about and ate individual leaves or twigs. Deer appeared to detect differences among individual leaves on the same plant by sniffing, licking or holding the leaves in their mouths before accepting or rejecting them. Preferences varied for individual plants of most species. In some parts of the study area yellow birch seedlings were browsed so severely that 3 and 4 year old plants were less than a foot high. On other parts of the area, yellow birch seedlings of the same age were several feet high and unbrowsed or lightly browsed. Several bramble patches were heavily browsed by both wild and tame deer and appeared to be highly preferred.'

The preferences of the deer could be assessed by comparing the percentage of time spent feeding on a plant with its abundance as judged by its percentage contribution by weight in sample transects. In this way high, medium or low preference categories could be ascribed to each species. High or low ratings were given when the difference between the percentage of feeding time and the percentage of weight was greater than one third of the percentage of the feeding time. A medium rating was given when

Table 7.2 Nutrient Composition (% Oven Dry Weight) and *in vitro* Digestibility of Samples of Deer Forage Through the Year.* The Samples were Collected from the Feeding Area of the Animals in Fig. 7.1

Class of forage and month of collection		Crude protein	Crude fat	Crude fibre	Ash	Nitrogen-free extract	Calcium
Mixed browse	May	16·2	3·1	19·9	6·0	54·8	0·8
	July	9·7	4·2	19·9	5·4	60·8	1·1
	Sept.	9·9	5·9	23·5	6·2	54·5	1·5
	Nov.	6·1	3·7	20·1	6·2	63·9	1·5
	Feb.	6·1	2·6	38·0	4·5	48·8	1·1
Mixed forbs	May	14·8	3·8	22·0	9·4	50·0	1·5
	July	11·4	6·0	26·2	6·8	49·6	1·2
	Sept.	9·4	5·0	26·6	7·3	51·7	1·3
	Nov.	7·9	4·8	28·2	6·4	52·7	1·3
	Feb.	14·0	2·8	12·7	21·0	49·5	1·3
Mixed grass	May	13·3	2·8	32·0	6·9	45·0	0·5
	July	9·4	3·0	33·3	6·5	47·8	0·4
	Sept.	12·4	2·6	32·6	6·9	45·5	0·5
	Nov.	7·2	2·1	32·9	7·8	50·0	0·4
	Feb.	14·8	3·1	19·0	14·9	48·2	0·4
Pine	May	9·2	5·0	32·8	2·4	50·6	0·2
	July	6·8	5·7	31·5	3·0	53·0	0·4
	Sept.	7·3	6·1	33·3	2·7	50·6	0·3
	Nov.	8·1	6·9	32·0	2·7	50·3	0·3
	Feb.	7·5	8·7	29·3	2·7	51·8	0·3
Lab ration (mean of five replications)		26·3	5·3	5·5	7·5	55·4	1·5
Mixed forage sample	May	16·4	3·3	25·4	7·9	47·0	1·0
	July	10·5	4·8	29·4	5·2	50·1	0·7
	Sept.	8·9	5·8	30·1	4·8	50·4	0·7
Acorns	Nov.	5·7	23·6	18·1	1·8	50·8	0·3
Dead leaves	Feb.	5·3	3·5	31·4	7·1	52·7	1·7

* Slightly modified from Short, 1971.

Phosphorus	Acid-detergent fibre	Cell-wall contents	Cell content	Acid-detergent Lignin	In vitro digestibility by deer rumen materials LAAP
0·3	27·1	32·1	67·9	9·9	33·1
0·1	27·0	33·8	66·2	12·0	31·3
0·1	30·8	37·1	62·9	11·1	30·8
0·1	28·6	31·9	68·1	16·1	25·8
0·1	46·0	56·8	43·2	18·6	25·4
0·3	29·3	34·3	65·7	6·5	36·9bc†
0·2	31·9	37·4	62·6	8·1	45·9ab
0·2	34·7	41·2	58·8	7·7	43·6ab
0·1	37·1	43·0	57·0	13·6	31·2c
0·3	—‡	31·3	68·7	—‡	48·7a
0·2	38·3	66·5	33·5	3·8	29·9a
0·1	39·9	66·7	33·3	4·9	30·6a
0·2	39·4	67·6	32·4	5·0	33·3a
0·1	43·9	70·8	29·2	9·2	19·3b
0·2	38·8	56·9	43·1	5·2	33·8a
0·2	36·2	45·1	54·9	13·4	26·7
0·1	39·2	45·1	54·9	16·4	28·7
0·1	40·4	47·1	52·9	15·9	27·1
0·1	39·3	46·3	53·7	19·6	24·1
0·1	36·9	41·1	58·9	14·9	25·0
1·0	7·2	13·0	87·0	2·0	67·8
0·3	29·6	44·6	55·4	—‡	38·4
0·1	34·0	45·3	54·7	12·0	32·2
0·1	36·4	46·9	53·1	13·6	33·9
0·1	21·6	27·7	72·3	10·8	27·0
0·4	36·1	49·4	50·6	23·3	13·5

† Values, within a food class sample for LAAP deer, followed by different letters are significantly different ($P < 0.05$).
‡ Analysis not available.

this difference was less than one third of the feeding time. A negative difference indicated a low preference.

The food preferences and the amount of time spent on each

Table 7.3 Percentage of Total Feeding Time Spent by Tame White Tailed Deer Eating Each Plant Species and the Degree of Preference for that Plant*

Forage	Winter	Early Spring	Late Spring	Summer	Early Autumn	Late Autumn
Herbaceous						
Ferns	8·8H	12·1H	1·3M	2·3L	4·6M	19·7H
Wild Oat Grass	3·9M	26·6H	7·2M	3·6L	1·8L	0·8L
Sedge	0·2M	8·2H	2·0M	5·0M	1·4L	4·3M
Dog-tooth Violet	—	16·1H	3·3M	0X	—	—
Spring Beauty	—	2·9H	0·4H	0X	—	—
Wood Sorrel	—	—	0·1X	1·9M	2·9H	2·2M
All Others	0·5X	1·1X	2·4X	1·8X	2·2X	0·2X
Subtotal	13·4	67·0	16·7	14·6	12·9	27·2
Tree and Shrub						
Yellow Birch	4·0L	1·9L	5·2M	10·0M	19·9H	8·5L
Beech	35·7H	3·3L	23·2H	6·3L	5·0L	6·8L
Black Cherry	2·4L	2·8L	3·8M	1·9L	5·3L	2·9L
Red Maple	1·5M	0L	1·2M	0·6L	0·9L	2·2M
Sugar Maple	2·2H	0·7L	10·2H	3·2M	0·8M	0·8H
Striped Maple	2·1H	0·9L	0·5M	0·8M	1·1M	2·5H
White Ash	0·7X	0X	1·3X	0·4X	1·2X	0X
Hophornbeam	0·2X	0L	0·5M	1·5H	0·6M	2·2H
All Others	0·1X	0·5X	0·4X	0·3X	1.0X	0·2X
Subtotal	48·9	10·1	46·3	25·0	35·8	26·1
Vine						
Brambles	19·0L	13·4L	31·3M	55·9H	37·8M	34·3L
Miscellaneous						
Fungi	1·6X	0X	0·3X	0·8X	5·5H	3·5H
Dead Twigs, Bark	3·4X	2·2X	0·2X	0·2X	0·5X	0·5X
Dry Leaves	9·4M	4·8M	0·7L	1·1L	5·8M	4·3M
Mineral Soil	3·4X	1·6X	1·9X	1·5X	0.9X	2·5X
Deer Faeces	0·2X	0·4X	0·8X	0·4X	0·4X	0·2X
Unidentified	0.7X	0·5X	1·8X	0·5X	0.4X	1·4X
Subtotal	18·7	9·5	5·7	4·5	13·5	12·4
Total	100·0	100·0	100·0	100·0	100·0	100·0

* Reproduced from Healy, 1971.

Fig. 7.7 The wolf, a major predator on northern species of deer, especially Reindeer and Moose, and formerly also on temperate forest species as well. Wolf numbers in many areas are now so small that they are no longer a significant predator on deer, and over much of western Europe they are no longer present.

species through the year is shown in Table 7.3 and in 7.4 the abundance and frequency of occurrence of the different plant species on the area are given.

It was found in this study that the deer ate 36 species of plant and in each seasonal period at least 87% of the feeding time involved only 10–12 species. The winter diet on snow-covered ground consisted primarily of twigs of trees and shrubs notably beech and bramble. As snow melted in early spring, feeding shifted to the new growth of ferns, grasses, sedges and forbs and this group accounted for 67% of feeding time. By late spring, attention turned to the growing shoots of trees, shrubs and bramble, the latter occupied 56% of feeding time in summer. In early autumn, bramble and trees and shrubs occupied 74% of the time and in late autumn, herbs, browse and bramble each made up similar amounts of the feeding time.

In Tables 7.3 and 7.4 it is interesting to see how one particular food plant is utilised at a particular time of year, wild oat grass and dog-tooth violet in early spring, beech in winter and late spring, yellow birch in autumn and bramble in summer.

In the more extreme environments it is advantageous for a

Table 7.4 Percentage of Feeding Time Spent by Tame White Tailed Deer on Each Plant

Forage	Winter			Early Spring		
	Feeding	Weight	Frequency	Feeding	Weight	Frequency
Herbaceous						
Ferns	8·8	1·4	45	12·1	5·0	65
Dog-tooth Violet	—	0	0	16·1	7·7	82
Spring Beauty	—	0	0	2·9	0·5	35
Wood Sorrel	—	0	0	0	0·1	9
All Others	0·5	0	0	1·1	3·3	35
Tree and Shrub						
Yellow Birch	4·0	8·3	95	1·9	7·0	71
Beech	35·7	22·1	91	3·3	35·9	63
Black Cherry	2·4	20·8	77	2·8	6·4	78
Red Maple	1·5	1·1	95	0	1·7	87
Sugar Maple	2·2	0·7	45	0·7	1·3	44
Striped Maple	2·1	1·1	41	0·9	0·1	5
White Ash	0·7	0·1	9	0	0	0
Hophornbeam	0·2	0	0	0	0·1	1
All Others	0·1	0	0	0·5	0·5	5
Vines						
Brambles	19·0	44·4	95	13·4	30·6	78
Total		100			100	

species to be able to eat many kinds of food plant as the opportunities present themselves. The Reindeer falls in this category,
with a wide range of plant species being taken. This contrasts
with the view that the Reindeer mosses—the ground growing
lichens of the genus *Cladonia*—are vital or even preferred,
apparent preference being a matter of availability. This is one of
several points made in a study of the food habits of Reindeer
(Caribou) in Newfoundland carried out by Bergerud (1972). The
influence of the environment on the food taken is well illustrated
as also is the degree of selectivity at certain times. This study

Species Compared to its Frequency and Mass*

	Summer			Late Autumn†		
	Feeding	Weight	Frequency	Feeding	Weight	Frequency
	2·3	9·2	67	19·7	—	—
	0	0·4	25	—	—	—
	0	0·1	5	—	—	—
	1·9	0·2	20	2·2	—	—
	1·8	7·6	76	0·2	—	—
	10·0	10·4	73	8·5	13·0	78
	6·3	17·2	69	6·8	20·4	64
	1·9	13·0	76	2·9	14·7	64
	0·6	2·8	96	2·2	1·9	92
	3·2	2·5	62	0·8	0·4	20
	0·8	0·9	11	2·5	0·1	5
	0·4	0·1	4	0	0	0
	1·5	0·6	29	2·2	0·3	4
	0·3	0·3	11	0·2	0·1	1
	55·9	34·9	84	34·3	49·2	92
		100			100	

* Reproduced from Healy, 1971.
† Herbaceous plants were not sampled.

Fig. 7.8 Western hemlock, growing in the British Isles as a commercial plantation softwood, stripped of bark by Fallow deer.

(Fig. 7.9) provides an interesting comparison with those of White Tailed deer described above.

In spring, following the thaw, the Reindeer sought out rapidly growing green plants taking very few lichens and bryophytes. The deer would feed on one species intensively then switch to another as it appeared. Larch needles and alder leaves were used briefly when they appeared in June and evergreen shrubs as they

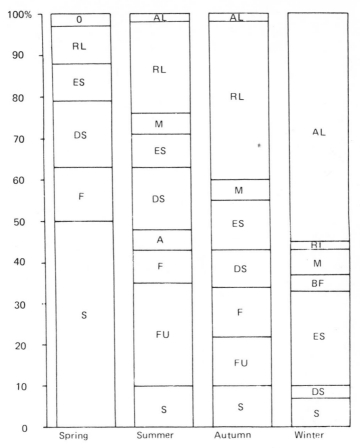

Fig. 7.9   Seasonal changes in the diet of Caribou Reindeer in Newfound-
land as indicated by the analysis of stomach contents. (Drawn from data
given by Bergerud, 1972.)
S = Sedges F = Forbs DS = Deciduous shrubs ES = Evergreen shrubs
RL = Reindeer lichens FU = Fungi A = Aquatic M = Mosses
AL = Arboreal lichens BF = Balsam fir O = Others

turned green prior to the appearance of deciduous growth.
Favoured plants included bunchberry, crowberry, blueberry and
Canadian burnet, but the most important plants were the sedges,
particularly *Scirpus* and some *Carex*. Summer offered the maximum
variety of food plants and all the major groups were used signifi-

93

Fig. 7.10 A Red deer hind with calf (at foot of picture), accompanied by a rutting stag. During the rut the stags, unlike the hinds, take little food and may lose quite a lot of weight and deteriorate in general condition.

cantly, including aquatic species. The latter together with moist lichens and fungi were increasingly taken in late summer.

In autumn, use of deciduous species declined rapidly with the leaf fall and the major food group was the *Cladonia* ground growing lichens, together with a mixture of each of the other feed groups. In winter, with the coming of soft snow cover in January and February, mobility was very much decreased until weight bearing crusts formed in March. Digging for lichens is difficult and there is a marked shift from ground lichens to the arboreal species and to evergreen shrubs, plus any other plant and tree species that could be gathered. With the disappearance of the snow, attention is rapidly turned to the new growth of sedges and forbs which are highly nutritious. Thus winter snow cover is a major influence on the feeding patterns of the Newfoundland Reindeer.

8 Antlers

Antlers are unusual and biologically very interesting. They are one of the fastest growing structures known in any animal and their growth involves a great deal of metabolic activity and mineral substance. What makes them even more unusual is the apparent extravagance and wastage of body tissue involved for they are not retained throughout life but are shed and regrown each year. A large Red deer weighing about 180 kg (400 lb) may grow antlers weighing 9 kg (20 lb) or more in about four months. The minerals involved are the same as used in bone formation and the skeleton of such a deer would weigh about 18 kg (40 lb). Each year, therefore, the mineral equivalent to half the weight of the skeleton is being mobilised to form the antlers only to be discarded a few months later and the cycle begun again. Antlers have attracted a great deal of attention in both popular and hunting literature and many bizarre explanations of their function have been put forward, including the idea that they are a store for surplus sex hormones! There have been a number of scientific investigations into the structure and function of antlers and various ideas as to their purpose have been put forward. These include their use for visual recognition, as rank symbols, in breeding displays, as fighting weapons and also a possible role as radiators to keep the animal cool in summer. The difficulty in explaining the function of antlers is simple enough, for the deer family has had antlers for millions of years. We are now looking at how the living descendants of these ancestral deer are using them today. The present method of use in a wide range of species cannot necessarily explain why these structures evolved or persisted, nor can we determine easily whether these are now biologically essential rather than just useful. In some species it may be that antlers come in the category of 'useful' rather than

Fig. 8.1   The White rhinoceros also has head appendages, but in this case the horns are composed of hair and are developed from the skin and not from the bone.

'essential'. In the Scottish Highlands, there occurs naturally an abnormality of a stag without antlers, called a hummel. This is a normal male animal in every respect but lacking antler growth. These hummels tend to be bigger and heavier than normal stags and are quite capable of holding a harem of hinds and of siring their offspring. If anything, in this harsh upland zone of largely acid soils, the hummel has the advantage over his antlered rivals in that he does not undergo the heavy physiological stress associated with the growing of antlers.

Many species of animal have elaborate structures on or about the head. These include birds such as the Cassowary and Hornbill, insects such as the Rhinoceros beetle and Stag beetle, reptiles including several species of chameleon—and among mammals there are the rhinoceroses and most of the antelopes, cattle, etc. In the past, many animals also had cranial appendages, e.g. dinosaurs like *Triceratops*. In human society it is the head area above all others which is elaborated and adorned. In many species these structures are more fully developed in one sex rather than the other, normally the male. The elaboration of such structures is not usually associated with the development of a physiologically more efficient structure such as increasing the size of the ear and its surface vascularisation in order to make a more efficient cooling structure. Rather, the role of these structures appears to be primarily located in the patterns of sexual behaviour, and to be used as part of a display to attract females and to intimidate rivals. It is therefore not difficult to see sexual behaviour as the likely reason for the development of antlers and other cranial embellishments.

Arising from the sexual role, it is perhaps almost inevitable that they would become involved in fighting. Many species of deer today carry large and elaborate antlers and there would, on the basis of social behaviour, be a natural selection for animals with the most elaborate antlers consistent with long term survival. We would expect, therefore, to see in the fossil record a tendency within the family to evolve forms with larger and larger antlers up to an optimum size. This indeed is the case and extinct species such as *Megaceros* represent the furthest recent development of this trend, almost matched by the living Elks (*Alces*) of North America.

The environment sets limits for such growths and this is well illustrated by the differences in amount of antler growth between deer on good and poor feeding areas. There is little comparison, for example, between the antlers of a Scottish hill stag and one from a lowland park or forest. Thus, the evolution of large antlers in certain species is probably due to the presence of more viable characteristics in animals with large antlers than in those with smaller ones. It is quite obvious that an animal that has survived to maturity and grown large antlers has shown himself to be a survivor rather than a younger one that, although fertile, is largely untested. Here perhaps also is the explanation of why antlers increase in complexity up to maturity, and why young males, who are fully fertile, are normally prevented by the social structure of the herd from breeding in the main breeding season, and why antler cycles have become synchronised with sexual ones.

The peculiarity of the antler structure lies in the fact that in temperate species it is grown and then shed every year. In some tropical species the cycle is thought to be of variable duration and of longer than twelve months. Periodic growth is not confined to deer but is common to the antelopes and their relatives the sheep and cattle. In these, however, the growth takes place in the horny sheath and not to the underlying bone. Why then have antlers evolved as structures which are cast and regrown and why is there a difference in the cycle between tropical and temperate species?

The ancestors of the deer lived in warm climates and the earth has been steadily cooling over the period of their evolution so that warm climates are now confined to the transequatorial areas. Tropical climates are characterised by nights and days of near equal length throughout the year, with no great temperature changes through the year. Rainfall provides the only clearly discernible climatic variable through the year. In contrast, the temperate regions are characterised by an annual cycle of considerable change in day length and of temperature and to some extent,

Fig. 8.2 Group of Hog deer at Whipsnade Zoo, England, in early June. The winter coat is still being moulted but the spots of the summer coat are visible. The bucks are all in velvet.

rainfall. The magnitude of the seasonal variation increases pole-
wards so that the more markedly seasonal and harsher regions are
found nearer the Poles. In temperate latitudes simple observation
enables one to determine the time of year; in tropical latitudes
this is not normally possible. In the tropics therefore, plants and
animals require an intrinsic timing mechanism and their timetable
can be flexible. Outside the tropics an internal clock is no longer
a necessity, but time-tabling must be regulated in order to keep
in step with the other environmental changes.

The antlers of the earliest deer probably never became fully
hardened but perhaps remained as firm living cartilage like structures covered by hairy skin. Probably also they were never shed
under the tropical regime. Coope (1968) has suggested that the
seasonal antler cycle developed because of changing climatic conditions. As temperatures got lower, those deer living in the north
would begin to suffer frostbite to the short antler points as a
result of which the tissue was killed and like all dead bone this
became separated by osteoclast (bone-eating) cells working at the
interface between live and dead tissue. Ultimately, the dead tissue
would fall away and be replaced by new growth from the wound
face.

This situation prevails in the antler cycle today. In the Red deer,
for example, antlers are grown from the permanent columnar
structures known as pedicles which are living, bony outgrowths
of the frontal bone of the skull. During growth the antler is
foetal bone, rubbery and richly endowed with nerves and blood
vessels and covered by the hairy skin known as velvet. At this
stage it is living. When growth is complete, the cartilaginous
tissue has become solid bone with a cancellous core and is devoid
of nerves and blood vessels and is no longer skin covered.
Effectively, the antler is dead bone as far down as the pedicle,
where just below the coronet is the live/dead interface. Now,
instead of osteoclast cells working at this face and separating the
two which is the normal tissue reaction, this process is delayed
for about 7–8 months when in the early summer osteoclast
activity begins and the antler is cast. Immediately, the skin grows
over the wound face and new antler growth proceeds.

One can therefore appreciate Coope's view that the periodicity of the antler rhythm was initiated by changing conditions, leading to seasonal climatic regimes in the areas occupied by many of the deer. This would necessitate quite a few changes in the physiological systems of these early deer to meet the new challenge of the seasonal environment. The changes that we are talking of cover something like twenty million years and span the globe. Our knowledge of these creatures in that time is enormously incomplete, so that proof of these theories is not available.

Not every form took the same course and, for example, we have the Roe deer which has an almost opposite timing of his antler cycle to that of other temperate deer. Equally, the more immediate ancestors of our tropical deer may in fact have evolved in temperate latitudes and re-colonised the Tropics. We are therefore faced with much uncertainty as to where, when, how and why these changes occurred. We can, however, study the variety found in the living forms and from these may postulate how certain events may have been effected or had advantages in the past. What we see now, however, probably arose under very different conditions and may no longer be relevant. In certain cases, we may observe structures or behaviour which are advantageous in changing environments, neutral or even harmful, and in the course of time these may well be modified, persist or even disappear.

Before going on to examine features of the antlers and their cycle in particular species, we shall look in a little more detail at how these structures are distributed in the family and then at the nature of their growth.

Of the forty or so species of deer, only the Chinese Water deer and Musk deer do not possess antlers. There is no evidence that these species ever had them. Antlers are the prerogative of the male except in the Reindeer, in which substantial antlers are normal in the female as well. Occasionally, the female of a species may develop small antlers, and in such cases it is probably due to some degree of hormonal imbalance. In the case of female Roe deer with antlers that I have examined, they have all been normal females and pregnant and this is the experience of most other observers—antlered females are mostly sexually normal in all gross appearances. More abnormal situations are theoretically possible, but have not been reported.

Examination of the area of the frontal bone where in the male the pedicles would be, reveals two interesting features. Firstly, in both male and female foetuses and young there is a mark at this site which as the hair develops, becomes the centre point of a whorl of hairs, which persists in the adult female but which is unravelled by the developing pedicle columns of the male and ultimately forms the hair covering of the pedicle. In young females, the bone here is smooth but in Roe, Fallow, Red, Sika and most other temperate species that I have been able to examine, a bump develops with age at what would be the pedicle site in a male and these can become quite prominent in older animals. In the female Rusa that I was able to examine from Woburn Park in England, a much more distinct pedicle, completely covered by skin, was present in all specimens and appeared to be a normal feature in the live females also. None of these, however, had any sign of antler growth.

The absence or abnormality of development of antlers is usually associated with damage to the hormone-producing glands. This is usually associated with testicular activity and the production, or otherwise, of the male sex hormone testosterone. Other causes may include abnormalities of the pituitary gland and also the parathyroid glands. Referring again to the Red deer antlerless variety known as a hummel, the stag appears sexually normal in gross appearance, behaviour and performance. Pedicles are present but antlers never develop. The nature of this strain is under investigation but numbers are few and study difficult.

The deer which is thought to most resemble the ancestral deer of Miocene times is the Muntjac. We can therefore reasonably regard this as a relatively primitive form of deer and one that is biologically extremely well adapted having survived with little change for so long. The antlers of the Muntjacs are small and simple, rarely having more than a single small branch from the main antler beam. The antlers are small and comprise less than 0·4% of the body weight. Other deer with small antlers and a similar low ratio of antler weight to body size include the Roe deer (0·6%) and the small Brockets, Pudu, etc. of South America. In fact, the small deer of the tropical forests have relatively much smaller antlers than the larger forms found in the temperate region. This relationship is also seen in the antelope tribe, where the small forest-dwelling Duikers of Africa also have relatively smaller horns than the larger forms such as Kudu and Sable antelope. This is presumably an adaptation to life in the bottom 75 cm (c. 30 in) of the jungle or scrub habitats.

The largest antlers are found in the deer of temperate latitudes and in terms of size, the largest are those of the Moose or Elk and may exceed 2 m (7 ft) in width. Moose are the largest of the deer and relatively there would appear to be little difference in size/weight ratio between these and the medium sized deer such as the Red, Reindeer, Sika deer, etc. It will be appreciated that the growing of these antlers is an immense physiological burden on the animal. This is not only a matter of the quantities of substance required, but also their nature and the rapidity of the growth. A big Red deer, for example, will grow around 9 kg (20 lb) of antler in 3–4 months. The structure of the fully formed antler is bone and the hard tissue of bone consists largely of calcium, magnesium and phosphorus, substances which are normally present in only small amounts in most foodstuffs. Within the body, these minerals are an intrinsic part of the skeleton and reserves can be established in the bones. The period of antler growth involves the removal of these minerals from the bone and their synthesis and deposition as part of the fabric of the growing antler. The daily mineral requirement for antler growth exceeds the normal daily ingested supply so that the balance is withdrawn from the bones. These deer experience a seasonal osteodystrophy comparable with osteomalacia of old age. This does not, however, appear to impair the animal in any obvious way. Clearly, there must be some threshold beyond which the body cannot deplete the bone mineral, or else spontaneous fractures would occur. One can, therefore, understand why the annual production of antler by an individual can vary in size and quantity, and why antlers tend to be smaller in areas of limited food availability and perhaps also on soils deficient in base minerals, as are many upland areas. However, this production by the male is not a unique feat for the female also metabolises large amounts of mineral from both food intake and skeletal reserves to feed the young.

There are differences in detail of appearance, timing and of development of the antlers and pedicles between the species. Most of those of temperate latitudes have a pattern essentially similar to that of the Fallow deer and this will be described as a general guide to the characteristics of antler development in this group. The general situation, as far as it is known, in tropical species appears to be essentially similar to that described for the Fallow deer. Yet I am not certain that the control mechanisms underlying these processes and cycles are the same between tropical and temperate forms, nor for certain whether they are the same in all temperate species.

In order to develop antlers in later life, deer must first grow the bony column or pedicles on the forehead from which the antlers develop. These are not present in the female and, thus, antlers are secondary sexual characteristics. They are developed only under the influence of the male sex hormone testosterone, which is secreted by the interstitial cells of the testes. If a fawn is castrated before the pedicles have begun to grow, it is normally incapable of developing either pedicles or antlers. If, however, testosterone is administered to the animal, pedicles will develop; and if administration is controlled appropriately, a cycle of growth, casting and regrowth takes place. Similarly, the administration of testosterone to female deer results in the growth of pedicles and antlers.

Pedicles are formed under the influence of the developing testes during the first year of life. In Fallow deer growth may begin any time from October/November till, exceptionally, as late as March, i.e. when the animal is aged about $4\frac{1}{2}$–9 months. In general, the smaller the animal, the later is the start of growth and the few late developers are likely to be animals born late in the season. The beginning of pedicle growth corresponds with an increase in the weight of the testes probably associated with the beginning of testosterone secretion by the interstitial cells. Once primed, the pedicles begin to form as an outgrowth of bone which is an integral part of the frontal bone. Throughout growth the pedicles are covered by hairy skin. The pedicle is fully formed by late spring/early summer, about the animal's first birthday, and growth of antlers follows immediately so that the first antler is grown in the second year of life (Chaplin and White, 1969, 1970, 1972).

The growing antler consists of cartilage-like tissue richly permeated by blood vessels and nerves from the covering skin, or velvet, as it is called. The velvet is covered by short hairs only a few millimetres in length. Growth occurs at the tip of the developing antler so that as the antler forms it is always of its final width. As growth proceeds at the tip by the laying down of new tissues, the existing cells are progressively ossified so that a section through a developing antler shows the whole succession of development from cartilage to bone from top to base.

When the antler is fully formed and ossification is complete, the blood vessels of the velvet constrict and the skin dries and comes away. This is a rapid process and the antler is usually free of skin tatters in a day or so. Because the growing antler is soft, it is easily deformed by knocks or bangs which may be partly repaired. Because of this, very few antlers have identical left and right sides. The growing antler is very warm to the touch and a great deal of heat is dissipated this way. As the growth is completed the antlers increasingly become itchy and the deer will rub them on thistles or plant stems. This rubbing as the skin finally dries up also serves to clean the antler and helps the deer to learn their shape.

Cleaning of the antlers occurs before the onset of the breeding season, at a time when the testosterone levels are rising sharply, and it may be that it is the rising testosterone level that signals growth to cease. In the absence of testosterone it has been shown that the antler will not harden in the normal way. Growth has taken approximately 3–4 months. The antlers fully formed remain in place until the following year when they are cast in the period April–June. It is the larger, older animals that cast first, followed within about eleven days by most of the sub-adults. It is my experience that the better the condition of the herd at this time, the earlier the herd, as a whole, will cast their antlers. Immediately after the antlers have been cast, exposing the raw surface of the pedicle, this dries and the skin that will form the velvet grows over the wound and the process of regrowth begins again.

The deer of the temperate latitudes follow a strict annual cycle, with mating and births occurring annually within a limited period of time. Most body functions are seen to relate to the season. The tropical deer like the Axis do not live in a seasonal environment and they do not exhibit any clear seasonality in their way of life. Instead, each individual appears to have its own internal cycles so that births occur at all times of year. Animals may be seen at all stages of antler development at any one time and there is little evidence of an annual cycle of antler development, or indeed of any regularity within it. In some populations there is, however, a certain amount of synchrony between individuals and at times this may suggest some seasonal influence. The physiology of these animals has hardly been looked at so that we know and understand little of the nature of such cycles. What is interesting is that when a herd is introduced to temperate latitudes, they do not adjust to an annual or seasonal pattern. Clearly, they have evolved a physiological system which does not respond to the external stimuli of the seasonal environment.

The Brown Brocket (*Mazama gouazoubira*) of northern South America has very small simple antlers and there appears to be no regular cycle of antler casting and growth. This species has been kept for many years in the Berlin Zoo and, despite the latitude, the antler cycle is similarly erratic.

However, at least one deer of the sub-tropical areas, the Reeves Muntjac has a control mechanism responsive to seasonal stimuli. As a result of introductions, this deer also flourishes in the British Isles. The antler cycle of this deer in its homeland—in southern China—is unfortunately not known. I have studied this deer in the wild and in captivity in the British Isles and found that the adult animals follow an annual seasonal cycle of antler growth, (Chaplin, 1972). The claim that in Britain the cycle of these animals is entirely intrinsic and unrelated to season, so that *adults* will be found at all stages of the cycle throughout the year, has not to date been substantiated by published data.

The pattern of the antler cycle is very similar in many temperate species. The Red, Fallow, White Tailed, Mule, Sika, etc. all grow the antlers during the summer, have them hard for the breeding season in autumn and cast them the following year in late winter/ early summer. Two temperate species have a very different timetable and present a rather fascinating picture of just how complex may have been the evolution of the antler and reproductive cycles.

Both, although more advanced than the Muntjacs, are regarded as primitive in comparison with say Red or Fallow deer. These two, the Roe and Pere David's deer, originated in Asia. The Roe has a transcontinental northern temperate distribution across Europe and Asia and has many points of resemblance with the White Tailed deer (*Odocoileus virginianus*) of the USA. The Pere David's deer originated from north-eastern China and in recent times became extinct in the wild. Its former distribution is only now becoming known from the bones found on archaeological sites and fossil remains.

Most Roe deer fawns are born in May or early June. The male fawn grows the antler pedicles during the autumn and these are fully formed in the New Year. Often a tiny cap or button of hard antler about 1 cm (0·4 in) high forms on top of the pedicle, and in spring this is cast. Not all animals grow this, but this small antler should be regarded as the first antler grown, even though some animals do not develop it. The second antler begins its growth in February–April and is completed and hard in July/ August, which is the breeding season. The antlers are then cast in October/November and growth of the new ones follows immediately. Thus, antlers are being grown through the winter and are hard in summer, the opposite to that found in most other species. In the species that grow their antlers in summer, the antler skin is covered by short hairs giving the appearance of velvet. In Roe, however, the skin is densely covered by long hairs, which serve to protect the growing antler from frostbite.

Just as this antler cycle is unique, so too is the reproductive cycle of the female. The explanation of those unusual cycles is discussed below and it seems that we are now seeing in the Roe deer the possible evolution of a different cycle.

The antler cycle of the Pere David's deer differs in its timing from that of Red and Fallow deer. The young are born in April/ May and the pedicles develop during the first year to be followed by the first antlers, which develop in the late summer of the second year. Unlike Red or Fallow deer, these simple spikes are not free of velvet for the July rut, but are usually cleaned of velvet during August and September and these may be carried well into late winter. In the adults, casting begins from October in the older

Fig. 8.3   Roe deer with antlers in velvet. The hair of the velvet is much longer than in those deer that grow antlers during the summer; the Roe grows them during the winter.

stags and is followed by regrowth of the antlers. These are fully formed and cleaned of velvet in May/June. Again the older animals are usually the first to clean.

Our knowledge of Pere David's deer is based almost entirely on the large herd at Woburn Abbey in Bedfordshire, England. The Pere David's deer were most closely studied by the Dukes of Bedford and there have been a number of changes in the cycle of these deer whilst at Woburn. In 1950, the Duke described these as follows:

'Adult Pere David's stags normally now begin to shed their antlers in October (originally they did so in September), but there can be great variation in the date of shedding from year to year. One season even the oldest stags carried their horns until after Christmas. As is usual with deer, the adults shed first and the younger ones later, in order of age, knobbers carrying theirs until late winter. The age difference is much less marked in respect of the date of cleaning, though the very first individuals to lose their velvet are always mature animals. After the antlers are cast, the new ones begin to grow at once, albeit slowly, and may take nearly six months to reach completion. When growing they appear to be less sensitive than those of other deer, for a stag may be seen to employ his still velvet covered horns to administer a gentle poke to a companion. Not many years after their arrival at Woburn, most of the adult Pere David stags (including the first imported) developed the curious habit of growing, during the course of twelve months, two small pairs of antlers instead of one large one. The summer horns would be shed in autumn, and by Christmas a short, simple pair, consisting of a back tine and terminal fork, would harden. These would be carried for a few weeks and then shed, in time to allow of the growth of another similar pair which would be cleaned in May. As a rule, stags showed no signs of sexual excitement when carrying their "winter" horns, but now and again one would begin to call and herd the hinds, though with less energy than during the proper rutting season. On one occasion, also, a stag which had just reached maturity and was carrying a large "single" pair of antlers was in full summer coat and calling and herding hinds in February, more than three months before the normal season. By way of contrast, I once heard a very late stag calling in mid-October, quite eight weeks after the end of the normal season. For some not very obvious reason, the habit of growing two pairs of antlers in twelve months has now almost entirely ceased and is of very rare occurrence. The change may have been encouraged, in the first instance, by under-feeding during, and after, the first World War, for a Pere David stag will not grow two pairs of antlers unless in very good condition.'

In the time I spent at Woburn Park, I never saw any evidence of this double growth. I was therefore rather surprised, on going to Edinburgh Zoo, to find that their stag, now at Calderpark, regularly produced two sets of antlers in a year—just as described by the Duke of Bedford. I am not, however, sure that it is feeding that is responsible for this. At Woburn, the deer have been maintained in good condition through the winter but two sets of antlers have not appeared. It is perhaps that this tendency was due to difficulties in synchronising the antler/reproductive cycle control system with the environmental triggers at this latitude. This

Fig. 8.4 Moose (Elk) with antlers in velvet.

would also explain the shifts in breeding season and calving date that have taken place since the deer were assembled in England and the fact that this has now been stable over the last 25–30 years.

A third variation in the cycle is exemplified by the male Reindeer and Moose. In these species the males cast their antlers after the late autumn rut and over winter there is no antler growth. Growth of the antler resumes in the spring. This has at least three advantages for the animal, which suggests that this type of cycle has evolved to cope with winter snowfall conditions and the problem this poses for survival. Damage by frostbite to the growing antler is avoided, as is the intense physiological stress of antler growth at a time of limited food supply. Thirdly, the absence of antlers ensures that the female is not at a disadvantage in feeding situations. The female Reindeer retain their antlers over the winter as do the calves so that these animals are generally dominant to antlerless males. This winter standstill would appear to be an adaptation to the especially harsh conditions encountered in northern continental climates.

The duration of each year's antler growth in adults shows significant differences between species. To be certain of this, it is essential to have a good sample of accurate observations of individual animals. Unfortunately, these are not readily available in any number, so some degree of approximation must be used. The growth period is here defined as the interval from casting both antlers to the date when a major amount of velvet stripping has occurred. A wild Sika stag required about 125 days, two Reeves Muntjac (Chaplin, 1972) took 104 days and 107 days, respectively, and one noted by Soper (1969) took 89 days. I estimate that Fallow, Red and White Tailed deer take about 120 days. A captive Roe deer took 120 days and the Pudu in the Berlin Zoo (see below) take 140–150 days in a full northern cycle (Frädrich, 1975). I do not know the significance of these differences. The contrast between Pudu and the Muntjac is particularly surprising considering the similarity in size of the antlers both actually and proportionately. On the other hand the Pudu are a very high latitude deer (approx. 38–45°S) and this may have a special influence in their particular habitat.

The Environmental Cue

In order to establish how antler cycles are regulated, a number of long-term experiments were undertaken in the USA. The problems of such experiments bear no relationship to those carried out on mice or rats in scientific laboratories. In contrast, they are difficult to perform, exceedingly expensive and usually beset by disasters. Often they must last many years. Not surprisingly, very few such large-scale experiments have been undertaken as the facilities and finance are rarely available.

Richard Goss (1969) of Brown University, Rhode Island, worked with Japanese Sika deer at the Southwick Wild Animal Farm at Blackstone, Massachusetts. Adult Sika deer mostly cast their antlers in May, grow new ones over the summer and harden and clean them during September. The year is defined by one complete cycle of increasing and decreasing day length. In order to determine whether or not the antler cycle of the Sika was regulated by the annual light cycle, a number of experiments were carried out. For these, the deer were kept in unheated barns, totally screened from natural light. Light was supplied from overhead fluorescent lamps. These lamps were automatically controlled in such a way that the light/dark cycle of a natural year could be followed normally, speeded up or slowed down. The machine was programmed for that latitude (42°N) but could also be adjusted for the conditions of other latitudes.

When at the start of the experiment a normal annual light cycle was imposed six months out of phase, the deer in due course adapted their cycle to the new calendar. Since this change went contrary to the temperature cycle, it showed that the antler cycle did adjust to changes in the seasonal light cycle and not to temperature. In the second experiment, the light cycle was speeded up two, three and four times to mimic in one actual calendar year the events of two, three or four years. After a period of adjustment to the cycle, the deer became more or less adapted to the new timetable. With a two-fold increase the deer usually grew two sets of antlers in the year, one in each artificial year cycle. The shortened growing season did not speed up the rate of antler growth, but led to the antlers being only partially formed. When the rate was increased to three seasons per year, three sets were grown but they were even smaller than on the two season year. When increased to four seasons per year, the deer first of all went through a cycle in each of the first two seasons, but in the third, growth was minimal and in the fourth there was no growth. In the fifth cycle antlers grew again. Finally, the deer were subjected to a run of two month years. The deer which had been newly brought in for the experiment followed the normal annual cycle of the natural environment and ignored the rapidly changing light regime of their new home.

These experiments suggested that the antler cycle follows the seasonal change in day length associated with a full year. When, however, the year was lengthened to twenty-four months, yearling animals adapted to the artificial cycle and produced antlers every two calendar years, the antlers stayed in velvet longer but did not grow any bigger than normal. The adult deer, however continued to grow antlers about every twelve months, irrespective of the prevailing light conditions.

This suggests that the underlying control mechanism of the antler cycle is an internal clock that is firmly locked on to the normal annual season, and while this can be made to run faster, it cannot be slowed down to anything like the same extent. The difference in response to the slowing down experiments between yearling and adult animals suggests that the programme for this internal clock becomes fixed only after completion of the first antler cycle.

In the Sika deer the speed of the clock has been set to correspond with the annual photo-period, so that the life cycle is fixed to coincide with the environmental year. Evolution has fixed this for survival in their natural environment which is a seasonal one. The interesting question is to what extent is this now fixed. Given an aseasonal environment or a different light regime, what would happen? Further experiments were done to find this out. In the previous series the amplitude of the cycle was that of $42°$ North defined by the Winter Solstice light/dark value of $9/15$ hours. The first experiment set out to determine just how little a difference between the length of day and night was reacted to by the deer. By varying the length of daylight in an accelerated year, it was established that the deer were responsive to a difference of as little as one hour between day and night lengths ($11\frac{1}{2}/12\frac{1}{2}$) compared to the equal length day/night $12/12$ of the Equator. This former figure corresponds to roughly latitude $9°$. It is interesting to note that this difference in day length is much less than that experienced by tropical deer in northern zoos who do not respond to the northern photo-period cycle. When the Sika deer were subject to a regime of equal lengths of night and day, $12/12$ as pertains on the Equator, the cycles of antler growth were halted. Fawns born into this environment grew their first set of antlers but never cast them. Yearling and adult animals which had already experienced the environmental triggers before introduction, completed the appropriate part of their cycle but thereafter never replaced their antlers normally. Some eventually lost them but the pedicle bones remained exposed and unhealed indefinitely. Thus, an equal length of day and night suppressed the antler cycle of the Sika deer. Further experiments showed that it was the fact of unequal day and night rather than a seasonal progression that was necessary for the cycle to take place. What did however happen was, that when maintained on a constant value for the inequality, synchrony disappeared and each animal began to cycle inherently. These cycles were not always a year in length.

Table 8.1 Antler Growth Cycle of *Pudu pudu* brought from Chile to Berlin*

Date of casting of first antler	Median date of cleaning velvet	Time antlers retained	Time taken to grow antlers
No. 1 Adult: arrived from Chile 14th October, 1969, with hard antlers			
16 March 70	18 June 70	unknown	115 days
18 Dec. 70	1 May 71	183 days	132 days
25 Dec. 71	—	238 days	—
No. 2 Adult: arrived from Chile 9th November, 1966, with hard antlers			
19 March 67	13 July 67	unknown	116 days
6 Jan. 68	—	176 days	—
2 Jan. 69	7 June 69	—	156 days
15 Jan. 70	6 June 70	221 days	141 days
14 Jan. 71	5 June 71	221 days	141 days
12 Jan. 72†	9 June 72	220 days	148 days
28 Dec. 72†	17 June 73	204 days	166 days
23 Dec. 73	22 May 74	189 days	150 days

* Data calculated from information supplied by Dr. Hans Frädrich, Zoological Garden, West Berlin.
† Normally both antlers were cast within a day or so of each other. In 1972 the left antler was cast 6 days after the right and in 1972 (December) this was cast 15 days later in January, 1973. This accounts for the apparent discrepancy in the duration of antler growth in those cycles.

One can summarise these results as follows.

The Japanese Sika deer is a northern temperate species. In this environment it has an annual cycle of antler growth which is synchronous with the season and with other members of the population. Experimental manipulation has, however, shown that the antler cycle is regulated by an internal clock that has become set at the annual seasonal rate because of the survival value of being in step with the environment. This clock can be speeded up or slowed down artificially. In an artificial environment where day and night are of equal length as at the Equator, the antler cycle is suppressed altogether, but even small inequalities $11\frac{1}{2}/12\frac{1}{2}$ hours between day and night length are responded to. In fact, as long as there is a difference between day and night length, the animals will cycle but become out of phase with one another. An annual cycle in synchrony with other individuals requires a cycle of variation in day/night length.

The fact of environmental regulation of the antler cycle in temperate deer is well established by these experiments. It has also been confirmed by observation of Red deer shipped from England to New Zealand and *vice versa*. These deer in due course adjusted their antler cycle to the season of their new home. The Pudu (*Pudu pudu*) of southern Chile and south-western Argentina also shows this phenomenon. When brought to Berlin they rapidly adapted their annual cycle to the northern timetable. The nature of this change, and the subsequent cycles of these animals, are indicated in Table 8.1 opposite, adapted from that recorded by Dr. Frädrich (1975) in the Berlin Zoo. The shorter growth and retention period of the first set of northern antlers will be noted.

The antler cycle of many of the tropical and sub-tropical species has not been adequately described from field observations over their whole range let alone under controlled conditions. Further, many commentators would appear to have been influenced by their knowledge of events in northern species.

Whitehead (1972) gives some information on antler condition for Sambar, Axis, Thamin and Swamp deer in Asia and of these Axis, Swamp and a further species, Rusa, have been kept in Britain.

Sambar in Central India (20°N) cast variably but mostly in the months of March and April. In Burma (20°N) casting is in May, June and July but in the Malay Peninsula (15°N–0°) casting of antlers and breeding becomes irregular. Animals may be seen with velvet, or hard antlers, throughout the year and this has led some observers to conclude that antlers are cast every two years. This is probably incorrect, it being more probable that casting is entirely irregular in the Malay Peninsula.

The Indian Axis are said to rut in April and May and to have the majority of calves in the period October–December. The majority cast antlers in August/September and grow new ones which are hard in March. These observations indicate an annual seasonal activity. Yet some authors record animals at all stages of the cycle through the year—and probably the above summary does not derive from a sufficient area of the species extensive range to pick up the possible variation. In the British Isles, captive herds of Axis breed throughout the year apparently without any sign of rut. Animals are seen at all stages of the antler cycle through the year and most observers agree that individual animals have their own non-twelve-month cycle. There may be a substantial degree of synchrony in some populations but I have yet to see any records for individual animals. (In case of confusion, elsewhere in this book I have regarded the Axis, in general, as a year round breeder in India and Ceylon.)

The Swamp deer of Central India (20°N) cast their antlers in May, but in Northern India (25–30°N) casting is in February and March and there appears to be a defined breeding season. In the British Isles, the Swamp deer rut in December and January and the young are born in the summer. Antlers are cast in spring/early summer.

The Rusa deer come from islands on or about the Equator and they seem to breed all the year round. At Woburn, however, the Rusa appear to have adopted a seasonal regime with a winter rut and summer births. White Tailed deer range from almost the Equator to around 50°N in southern Canada. The antler cycle varies over this range as does the breeding season. In the northern part of this range antlers are cast during the winter and have an annual cycle of development. In South America there is apparently no distinct seasonal cycle. Bucks at any stage of the antler cycle can been seen all the year round. This is in accord with the experimental evidence described above, which indicated that below about 9°N the difference between the length of day and night was insufficient for the regulation of a synchronous seasonal cycle. The South American populations of the White Tailed deer lie to the south of latitude 11°N, and under these environmental conditions it was shown that animals would follow an entirely endogenous individual cycle. Thus, the field observations are in full accord with the experimental results.

From these examples, it seems likely that most of the subtropical species have a considerable elasticity in their cycles which are fixed by local conditions. Where ranges extend from seasonal to aseasonal environments, it is to be expected that a species will exhibit patterns which differ between them. In Rusa, which are Equatorial in origin, it would appear that like other members of the genus *Cervus*, they are able to adapt to seasonal environments. In contrast, the Axis seems to lack this ability.

Hormonal Controls

Whilst the cycles of antler growth are programmed by the light regime the stages of the cycle are under hormonal regulation. Hormones are chemical signals produced by the endocrine glands which circulate through the body and are reacted to by target organs. Hormones may start, stop or alter the rate of operation of the target organ. Overall control of the hormonal system is effected by the pituitary gland, a small gland 1–2 cm (0·4–0·8 in) in length located beneath the brain. The pituitary controls the secretory activity of other glands and organs.

In considering the regulation of the antler cycles, we are concerned with the pituitary as the master controller and with the interstitial cells of the testes which produce the bulk of the male sex hormone testosterone. Our knowledge of hormonal production and control is very limited and a great deal of research is being done. Unfortunately, substances and mechanisms are not always the same in different animals and very little work has been done, or can be done on hormonal regulation in deer because of the huge costs involved. It is only recently, for example, that two hormones concerned with calcium regulation have been discovered, calcitonin in the thyroid gland which lowers blood calcium levels, and parathormone in the parathyroid gland which raises blood calcium levels.

I am quite certain that our present view of hormonal controls of antler growth will be greatly expanded in the future. The experimental work described below has all been carried out on the seasonal deer of the temperate latitudes. It may possibly be found that the mode of action of the hormones is different even between these species and probably also very different in the subtropical species of deer.

In the temperate species work has tended to suggest that the antler cycle is interlocked with the cycle of the reproductive organs. My own work (Chaplin, 1970, 1972) suggests that at least in Fallow deer this could be misleading. The two cycles are closely correlated but are not necessarily functionally interlocked.

The annual changes in the antlers of the Red deer are influenced by the testes, the interstitial cells of which secrete the hormone testosterone. During the first nine months of life, the testes must produce an initial secretion of testosterone in order to stimulate growth of the pedicles, without which antlers cannot be grown.

As stated previously, if a young Red or Fallow deer is castrated, pedicles will not develop and antlers will therefore never grow. If, however, testosterone is administered pedicles and antlers will develop. Thus, an initial secretion of testosterone is essential to initiate the cycle. If an adult stag with hard antlers is castrated, the antlers are cast in about three weeks. Growth of new antlers commences at once, but the antlers are inferior in size and shape to those of an intact animal. They grow for longer than the usual period of time—around four months. They never harden and remain in velvet for the rest of the animal's life. Equally, if the animal is castrated whilst in velvet, growth continues for a while but finally ceases. If testosterone is administered to these castrates in perpetual velvet, the antler hardens and the skin is shed. Subsequently, the antler is cast and a new one is grown to the velvet stage. This reaction to castration appears typical of temperate species having been established by several workers in Red, Fallow,

Sika and Roe deer. In Red, Fallow and Sika deer, I believe that there is little or no further velvet growth in subsequent seasons. In the Roe deer, however, it appears that some new velvet is formed by a castrate in each summer season. It is this growth that leads to the grotesque type of velvet antler formations known as perruque heads.

The antler situation in the Reindeer is unique in many respects. Of interest here, however, is the fact that castrated reindeer retain a normal antler cycle even though in size and form the antlers are inferior to those of the male. Since female Reindeer have an annual antler cycle this is perhaps not surprising.

In a study of the Red deer on the Scottish island of Rhum testosterone levels were measured at various stages of the cycle through the year (Lincoln, Youngson and Short, 1970). These measurements establish threshold values for the action of testosterone in the normal adult cycle. Growth of the first antlers follows immediately that pedicle growth is completed in the spring and at a time when testosterone levels have never yet been high. The antlers grow over the summer in the presence of minute testosterone levels. In late summer, testosterone secretion increases and above 18 mg/100 g the antlers harden and the velvet is shed.

Hypersecretion of testosterone during September and October induces rutting behaviour at levels in excess of 100 mg/100 g and levels of over 400 mg/100 g were found at this time. Testosterone. levels fall sharply after the rut, overwintering levels vary between individuals but secretion is undetectable only in April, May and June, the time when the antlers are shed and regrowth commences. It would seem that even minute amounts of testosterone may inhibit antler casting, so that almost total quiescence of the secretory cells or their removal (by castration) is necessary to induce casting.

Testosterone levels should not be confused with libido. The stag has libido all year apart from a period of quiescence in May/June. The rut is a period of intense sexual activity, effected by a brief period of hypersecretion of testosterone. Rutting behaviour is not normally apparent outside of this time, but is easily stimulated by a hind in oestrous.

In both Red and Fallow deer, antler casting does occur in the brief period of sexual quiescence, as judged by both hormonal levels and spermatogenic activity. In the Reeves Muntjac in the British Isles, however, antlers are cast in May/June when the animals are sexually active. The testes are actively producing sperm and are no smaller than those of animals with hard antlers at this or other times through the year. This species does not appear to have a hypersexual rutting period, for although there is a diffuse seasonal pattern of births, the animal is not known to change its behaviour or appearance at any special time as is the case with deer that do rut. It seems possible, therefore, that the antler cycle is not under the control of the testes in quite the same way as in Red and Fallow deer, although it must be acknowledged that testosterone levels have not been monitored nor have castration experiments been reported for this species.

The normal antler/reproductive cycle of the temperate latitude deer has evolved over a long period. Since, in the past, the ancestors of our modern deer may have come from sub-tropical latitudes, and also past climates were warmer than now, it is probable that the cycles have evolved from systems present in the ancestors but adapted to cooler temperate conditions. The intriguing question is, what was the primitive control system and does it still survive in any of the living species of those regions? Is there in fact any need at all for tropical deer to have an antler cycle?

Why Antlers?

A variety of functions has already been ascribed to the antlers of deer including that of acting as a store for surplus sex hormones. It has, however, been well established that today the role of the antlers in deer is largely a social one. This is certainly true of the temperate species with relatively large antlers and is closely correlated with their further use as weapons. This social role is considered below. Information on the use of smaller and simpler antlers, such as those of Pudu and Muntjac, is limited and their role is much less clear than in those species with relatively large and complex antlers.

Before examining the social roles there is a further theory of

Fig. 8.5 The antlers of the Pere David's deer are growing during the winter and the hair of the velvet is long and woolly.

antler function that merits attention. This was set out by Stonehouse (1968) and was based on measurements of heat loss by the antlers in velvet. In essence, the theory is that a significant function of the velvet antler is to act as a radiator. Although, as a general function of antlers, this theory is not acceptable, heat loss could be an important element in recent physiological adaptations in some species.

The velvet of temperate species such as Sika and Fallow deer and of tropical species is thin and well supplied with blood vessels. These species grow their antlers under favourable climatic conditions, whereas those like the Roe and Pere David's (which grow antlers during the winter) are well insulated with long hairs. Heat loss and conservation are therefore of survival significance to at least some members of the family.

The growing antler has an extremely good supply of blood with a surprisingly dense plexus of vessels located in the velvet. This superficial distribution of vessels leads to a great deal of heat loss and a growing antler is very warm to the touch. In summer, no doubt, the radiator cooling effect is very welcome and the well-

Fig. 8.6 Scottish Red deer stags fighting with their antlers during the autumn breeding season.

grown antler represents a temporary increase in body area. In real terms it would correspond to roughly an extra pair of legs, but in cooling efficiency, a great deal more.

The role of antlers in social behaviour is best seen in a species such as the Red deer where there is a very strong social organisation (Darling, 1937). In Red deer the size and condition of the antlers affects the rank of an individual in the herd, determines the type of aggression displayed and serves for individual recognition. During the rut they are used as weapons. In Red deer the young and mature stags live in all male groups for most of the year separate from the females. These groups commonly consist of up to twenty individuals and break up during the rut, re-forming later.

Dominance, once established, is asserted by a graded series of head movements by antlered stags. This can vary from a slight movement or flick of the antlers to more savage prods. If the offending animal does not respond, i.e. he challenges the other, the intensity of display is increased and can ultimately escalate into an actual fight. This is an exceptional state, as the function of a dominance hierarchy is to reduce clashes in a group.

Dominance, once established, is rarely contested except when the groups reform in November after the rut. As the antlers are cast rank may change and although position is normally maintained it may well be challenged by previously subordinate animals who still have antlers. There is generally a tendency for the prime large antlered stags to be highly ranked and it is these that normally cast their antlers ahead of younger animals. Thus, at casting, the subordinates have a brief period of authority. Once an animal has cast he is very conscious of his inability to assert rank and this is true for the whole of the herd. When the herd is in velvet there is only a limited acceptance of dominance and this can be readily challenged whatever an animal's position was in the antler hierarchy. Contestants at this time do not use the antlers but instead box with the forefeet.

Antlers are not the sole determinant of status as was demonstrated by the removal of antlers from a relatively highly ranked male. He in fact remained dominant to most of the younger animals. The antlers also serve for the recognition of individuals and unfamiliar animals approaching a herd may well be attacked. In the Rhum experiments, individual animals antlers were modified either by the removal or addition of tines. When the stag returned to his herd he was not at first recognised by the others and was threatened.

This type of use of antlers seems to hold true for many other species. Although I have never studied this closely, general observations of Fallow, Sika, Axis, Pere David's, Rusa, etc. suggest that antlers are used in a similar way in social situations.

The survival value of dominance is by no means straightforward and herd and individual interests may not be the same. A rank order system within social species has been evolved as part of a behavioural/physiological/ecological complex. The heavy mortality found amongst yearling males in almost every deer species in temperate regions is a major natural cull. Any animal that survives the vicissitudes of the early years is a winner and one that does so and at the same time grows well and develops large antlers is biologically successful. It is these genes that have the greatest survival value for the herd, so that it is not surprising that a rank order system has evolved that favours the survival of proven animals and which tests others.

In Red and Fallow deer the male and female herds occupy different ranges except during the rut (Chaplin and White, 1970; Darling, 1937; Lincoln, Youngson and Short, 1970). There is thus no competition between male and female for food that could prejudice species survival. In nature the two herds do not interact on winter range. In a deer park where there is winter feeding the sexes must be fed separately otherwise all antlered males are dominant to the females and young who would get no food. Equally, food must be well spread for both male and female herds otherwise dominant individuals would get most of it.

In Reindeer, however, this potential conflict does arise with males, females and young sharing common winter grazing. The antler cycle, however, is different between the sexes and this can be explained in relation to the survival advantages it offers for the species at the expense of the individual (Henshaw, 1969). This cycle also prevents excessive energy loss from the radiator effect of growing antlers and damage from frostbite.

In winter, when the ground is covered with snow, Reindeer feed on lichens which they expose by digging craters in the snow with their feet (not with their antlers). Not only do females have antlers, but the calves also develop them before the onset of winter. Studies on Reindeer showed that those with antlers are dominant to those without. Winter is the critical time for this species and, providing snow depth and condition is not exceptionally difficult, the most testing time is the end of winter before the spring thaw. Male Reindeer cast their antlers before the turn of the year and will not begin to grow new ones until spring is under way. Females and fawns of both sexes retain their antlers through the winter. Non-pregnant females cast theirs before pregnant females, who normally do so within about a fortnight after calving. Thus, for most of the winter, adult females that can dig for their own food are dominant to the males, as are the fawns, and these can both dig their own craters, occasionally displace males from theirs or at least share the grazing. The greatest de-

Fig. 8.7 Red deer stags fighting with their feet. This form of fighting is only used when the antlers are in velvet. The stag on the left has cast his antlers and the new growth has begun, that on the right has not. This is scrapping within the stag group during the spring.

mand for food for finishing the foetus, producing the milk and ensuring the survival of the mother comes at the onset of Spring at the time of greatest shortage. By casting earlier, non-pregnant females leave the way clear for the pregnant females to become dominant in feeding situations, thus ensuring the well-being of the potential young and the best chance of survival of the species. This type of adaptation is only appropriate and feasible in polygamous herd species.

It is not certain what the social implications of antlers are in a deer like the Roe. Here, the bucks are growing antlers during the winter and bucks and does share the same ground. Social organisation consists not of a herd of recognised individuals in a herd territory but of smaller non-herd units of males, females and juveniles within some sort of territory range. Who or what defines this, or the relationship between the individuals in it, is not at all clear. Recent Roe deer research with marked individuals has, however, suggested that traditional views on this may be completely erroneous and attempts to derive a social function for the antlers could be misguided. In species which are more solitary, like the Muntjacs, the social role of the antlers is probably limited and they would appear to be used more as weapons and in territory marking. It is interesting that the largest antlers are found in the social species and the smallest in non-social species like the Roe, Pudus and Muntjacs.

There are a number of interesting and curious ways in which the antlers are used by particular species and these are probably of secondary origin. Scratching is not a major function of the antlers, but there is no doubt that large antlers are greatly appreciated for getting to those irritating places that nothing else can!

During the period of the rut when the males are aggressive there is much thrashing of vegetation—tall grass, branches, bushes, etc. as a displacement activity. Two species, however, Pere David's and Manchurian Sika, take this further and deliberately accumulate vegetation on the antlers to make them more impressive.

Scent is an important means of communication in deer and the antlers are involved in this. The growing velvet is skin and could possibly possess secretory cells producing an odoriferous substance. Keraman Sika have a very oily almost hairless black velvet and some other species have slightly greasy velvet. The significance of such secretions by the velvet are entirely unknown and may, in fact, be 'sunburn' oil to protect the skin, or even an insect repellant against the many blood sucking insects that would feed on the velvet. I have never, for example, seen ticks on the velvet.

The scent disseminated by the hard antlers is, however, produced elsewhere on the body and I know of two, possibly three, sources for this. The first is urine. Rutting males can produce fluid via the penis to order and this is done frequently in a variety of circumstances. I call this fluid urine + because it undoubtedly contains other substances. Urine + is odoriferous and it may be applied directly to the ground in a scrape made by the antlers or forefeet; sprayed over the lowered head, legs and underside of the body by rotating the penis in a controlled manner; or by spraying into a churned mud or wet patch and then rubbing the antlers or the body in the wallow. In this way urine + is well spread around and can be smelt at a distance by even a human nose. The feet are often used to stir up these wallows and it is possible that secretions from the interdigital glands if present might also be added. The other main gland would seem to be the metatarsal gland where present as deer are often seen rubbing the metatarsal bone with the antlers. This is not proven and could be mere scratching; what ever the purpose though, any secretions would be spread. The antlers then disperse the perfume either on the wind or transfers it to trees and bushes, ground scrapes, etc.

9 Reproduction

Much of the adult life of deer is concerned with reproduction and this is one of the fundamental drives within all the species. Many factors can influence the reproductive activities of both male and female at all stages of the cycle, and these influences fundamentally affect not only the individual, but the population as a whole. A knowledge of the nature of reproduction and of the factors which influence it are basic to an understanding of the life of deer. Reproduction is controlled by both internal and external factors and in this section we examine these and their interaction.

Well before either a male or female reaches physical maturity, the sexual organs are developing under the influence of various hormones secreted by the endocrine glands and these organs become functional and the animal can participate in sexual activity, if allowed to do so by social forces. This means that in the males the testes are producing spermatozoa, which collect in the tube called the *vas deferens* and which leads from the main storage organ, the epididymis, to the penis. Other organs associated with this are also producing the secretions which make up the ejaculate. Many other secondary characteristics such as a thickening of the neck are developed for the first time and specific sexual behaviour appears in its proper context. Some deer remain sexually active all the year round but most have only a short breeding season—the rut—and are not normally sexually active the whole year round.

The female, in contrast, is involved in reproductive activities for most of the year. Puberty is reached before maximum body weight is achieved and in some species can be delayed if growth has been so poor as not to reach a threshold of nutrition and weight. Conversely, in very good conditions puberty may be advanced. The sexual cycle in the female consists of the release of one or more

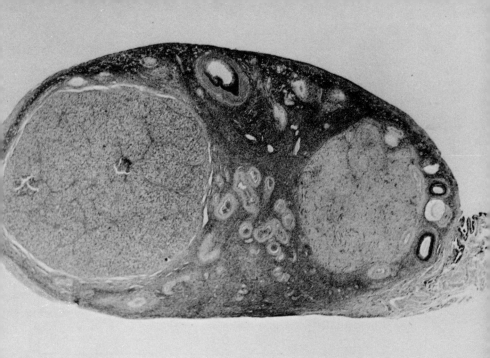

Fig. 9.1 Photomicrograph of a section through the ovary of a Muntjac deer. A large *corpus luteum* fills the left-hand side of the ovary indicating that the animal had either recently ovulated or was pregnant. A degenerating *corpus luteum* is present on the right, indicating that the deer had ovulated some weeks before but had failed to become pregnant.

eggs from either or both of the ovaries (ovulation), these eggs pass into the fallopian tubes where they meet the spermatozoa from the male and fertilisation occurs. The fertilised eggs begin their development and pass into the main body of the uterus. It is here that the developing embryo establishes contact with the mother through the development of the placenta and continues its development to term. Following ovulation, the follicle in the ovary from which the eggs was released forms into a body of yellow-coloured cells (called a *corpus luteum*) which secretes the hormones which will maintain the pregnancy and prepare the uterus. If, for any reason, the eggs are not fertilised, the *corpus luteum* degenerates and a new series of follicles ripen in the ovary, Ovulation will again occur and the animal comes into heat. Most deer conceive at the first oestrous and it is unusual to find more than two heat periods in a season.

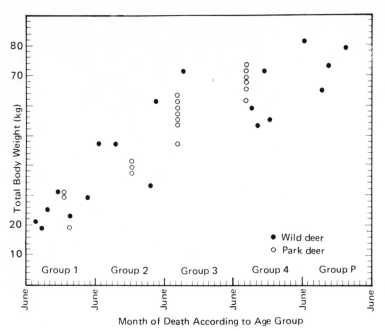

Fig. 9.2   Growth of Fallow deer bucks as indicated by total body weight in relation to year age group and month of death. For the Park deer, animals in Groups 1 to 4 are considered to be their first to fourth years, respectively, and Group P animals are in their fifth or subsequent years. (Redrawn from Chaplin and White, 1969.)

That is the basic cycle of events. The underlying physiological processes are essentially similar in most of the species so far studied. What is different, however, is the way in which each species has modified these processes to adapt to its particular environment. Below we examine in more detail a selection of species to examine how each has adapted.

The Male

The Fallow deer of Europe and the Mediterranean region is of medium size and exhibits a marked autumn rut and a restricted season of summer births. It has been extensively studied by the

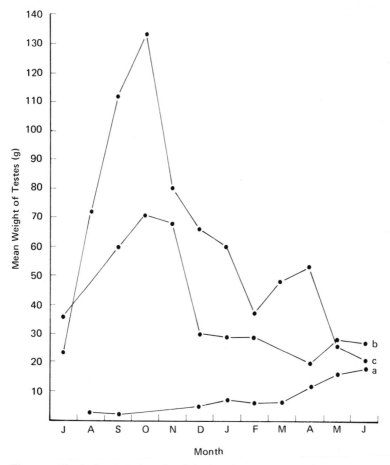

Fig. 9.3   Testicular growth and activity in relation to age and season in Fallow deer in the British Isles. (Redrawn from Chaplin and White, 1972.)

writer in both the field and laboratory, and is an ideal subject to illustrate the events in such animals (Chaplin and White, 1970, 1972). Fig. 9.2 shows the total body weights for a sample of Fallow deer according to age and month of death. This arrangement indicates the trend of increasing body weight with age and also the degree of variation to be encountered amongst normal healthy animals (Chaplin and White, 1969). In Figs. 9.3 and

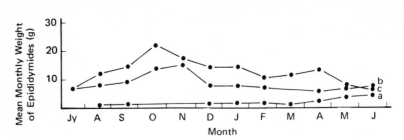

Fig. 9.4   Changes in the weight of the epididymides in relation to age and season in Fallow deer in the British Isles. (Redrawn from Chaplin and White, 1972.)

9.4 the average weight of the testes and the epididymides are similarly plotted. Three features emerge from this plot:

1   A period of initial growth of the testes and epididymides;

2   An annual cycle of increase and decrease in weight superimposed on

3   An increase in weight and amplitude with age up to maturity.

The fawns are mostly born during June. For the first four months of life, the testes are very small, weighing under 2 g (0·07 oz) each, but from November there is a gradual increase in weight so that at about ten months some may have testes weighing about 16 g (0·56 oz) but others are small weighing 5 g (0·18 oz) or less. The increase in weight, however, continues unchecked into the second year and a peak weight occurs during the rut. Thereafter, the weight of yearling testes declines rapidly to remain at between 10 and 20 g (0·35–0·70 oz) from December to June. Hereafter, there is an annual seasonal cycle of growth and regression of testicular weight as seen in older animals, but the testes also increase in overall size with age. In this respect, the testes follow the trend of overall body weight. Body growth in males is rapid in the first to third years and slower thereafter—animals probably reach a maximum body weight between four and six years. The growth of the epididymis parallels that of the testes.

The testes contains numerous coiled tubules lined by the cells, which produce and nourish the developing spermatozoa which subsequently migrate down the tubules into the epididymis and

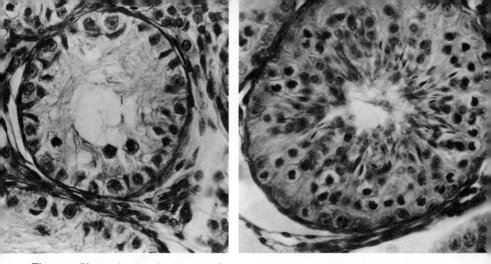

Fig. 9.5 Photomicrographs (× 360) of the seminiferous tubules of the
testes of adult Fallow deer, showing the seasonal changes in activity.
Left From an adult killed in early summer. The tubules are lined only by
a single layer of spermatocytes and spermatogenesis is inactive.
Right From an adult killed in late summer at the start of the rut. The
tubules are much larger and the spermatocytes are active. The various
stages in the development of the spermatozoa are present and the most
advanced stage in their production is represented by the dark cylindrical
bodies laying close to the centre of the tubule. The spermatozoa migrate
through the tubules into the epididymis where maturation occurs.

vas deferens. To establish the stage of activity of the testes, thin
sections were cut and stained and examined under the microscope. These studies showed that production of sperm in the
tubules (spermatogenesis) commenced towards the end of the
first year and that full spermatic production was reached during
the rut in the second year of life (i.e. at about 16 months). The
decline in testes weight is associated with a declining production
of spermatozoa. In adults, production has normally ceased by
March and in most animals there is a period of quiescence before
spermatogenesis is again stimulated any time between April and
June. A fertile mating is dependent on the presence of adequate
amounts of spermatozoa and of the secretions of the accessory
glands. Spermatozoa are first found in the epididymides of yearlings from mid September but in older animals they are present
from mid-August. Spermatozoa persist in the epididymides of
younger animals until mid to late February and in older animals
as late as April. These must represent the outside limits of the
period when fertile matings could occur. The effective period for

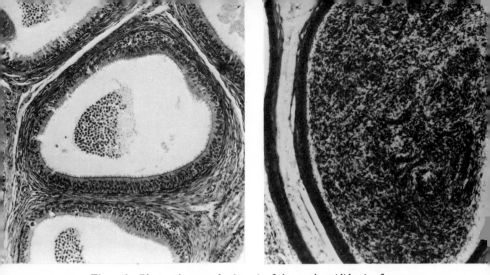

Fig. 9.6 Photomicrographs (× 90) of the *cauda epididymis* of mature Fallow deer. The epididymis is a long coiled tube in which the spermatozoa are matured, stored and nourished. Spermatozoa only appear in quantity in the epididymis some time after their production has commenced in the testes. Spermatozoa are present in the epididymis long after the production by the testes has declined or ceased, so that as long as these remain abundant, viable late matings can occur well outside of the normal breeding season. On the left, the first production of the testes is beginning to appear in the tubules of a yearling buck approaching his first rut at the beginning of September. On the right, the tubules are greatly enlarged and are packed with millions of spermatozoa. In Britain, this is the condition at the onset of the rut in late September/October in this seasonal breeding deer.

mating is, however, probably only September–February since both the volume of secretion and the concentration and motility of the spermatozoa are critical factors.

Characteristic of many deer like the Fallow is the limited breeding season accompanied by a period of hyperactivity known as the rut (Chaplin and White, 1970). There is both a build-up and decline from the breeding season in the population as a whole but for individuals the rut is a period of hypersexual activity during which behavioural factors influence the number of actual matings. The period in which a male is in rut should not be confused with the much longer period over which a male has libido and is fertile. Sexual activity can be aroused late on in the breeding season by the appearance of oestrous females, but it does not precipitate the same intensity of activity.

There is ample evidence that in medium to large deer with an autumn rut puberty is reached as a yearling. There seems little point in splitting hairs over the definition of puberty. Even if older males prevent a yearling from actually mating in the normal social situation they will, without competition, successfully mate with the females. In the wild there will often be situations when yearlings do cover adult females and, indeed, yearlings are often the largest sexually mature cohort in the population and have a significant part to play in mating the female herd.

In Fallow deer in the British Isles, we do not have the same kind of over-stocking of range and winter starvation as is sometimes encountered in the USA, with, for example, White Tailed deer. Here, even if the first winter is tough for the fawn, there is ample time to put on condition and make good some of the loss before the onset of the rut. Puberty can still be attained during the rut even if it is a few weeks later than in better nourished ones. In deer parks, however, one sometimes sees the beginnings of the effects of over-stocking when winter coats are retained into early June and testicular growth has not recommenced. These are, however, matters of degree and do not give rise to anomalies in attaining puberty. Because there are only a few months between birth and the autumn rut, Fallow fawns are not known to exhibit abnormal precocity. In certain situations, the larger Red deer calves kept under exceptionally good conditions have produced viable sperm as fawns as vouched by successful matings. These are abnormal situations but their value lies in indicating the potential of the animal as compared to what is possible in the natural environment. Early puberty seems to be a matter of being in adequate condition to respond to the environmental cues that trigger the rut. The further on in the year the rut occurs, the more chance there is that precocious animals may reach puberty within the fertile period. In White Tailed deer in the USA, it is likely that in areas of good nutrition there will be animals reaching puberty in their first winter. In contrast, the incidence of the breeding season in Roe deer (July/August) following May/June births effectively guarantees that no Roe fawn will join the summer rut. There are, however, many very strange physiological and behavioural happenings in Roe deer in the period November–February and it is possible that some male fawns, and perhaps also adults, are sexually active at this time. This is speculation at the present time, but the question is under active investigation.

The Chinese Water deer is precocious in almost every respect compared to other deer since it develops so rapidly and gives birth for the first time at one year of age. Fawns in Britain are born in May/June and both males and females are sexually active during the rut in December although both increase their size and certain other secondary sexual characteristics as yearlings. The large series of animals that I have examined indicate that puberty for all animals occurs at about 4–7 months and this is confirmed not only by examination of the gonads but also from controlled breeding experiments.

Where there is no fixed breeding season it is not so easy to establish puberty since this is a property of the individual and the environment to a much greater degree than in the temperate seasonal breeders. Studies of the Reeves Muntjac show that despite an apparent diffuse seasonal pattern of births, the males are fertile all the year round and there is no seasonal fluctuation in weight or activity of the testes nor a period of rut. The same would seem to be the case with the Axis. Yet, rather surprisingly, the Swamp deer which lives in the same part of India has, in the British Isles, a winter rut.

In other deer it was noted that the pedicles were normally fully formed before puberty. However, this is not the case in Muntjac, for one animal in which these were still developing showed full testicular activity. It is not certain whether in this species puberty relates more closely to actual age or whether the age at puberty is determined by both calendar age and the time of year. If the latter were the case there would probably be a wide range of age over which puberty occurred. There is, however, insufficient data to settle this point at the present time, although the indications are that the male Muntjac becomes fertile at less than a year, most likely at 6–9 months.

In the seasonal breeders, the lead up to puberty is the first indication that the fawn is now in synchrony with the annual seasonal cycle. Hereafter, the reproductive cycle will be under the influence of environmental triggers mediated by the pituitary gland. Responses to these stimuli will be only slightly modified in relation to individual circumstances. In succeeding years there will be an annual cycle of growth and regression of the testes and other seasonal sexual characters such as the mane. In those with no marked seasonal breeding, spermatogenic activity is maintained all through the year.

Thus, in male deer two distinct patterns of testicular activity emerge, on the one hand some have a limited period of fertility frequently characterised by a hyperactive phase of rutting, and others are fertile all year round and there is no rutting period. In the seasonal breeders, the antler cycle is correlated with the sexual cycle but in the aseasonal breeders there is no difference in testicular activity in relation to antler condition.

The Female

The breeding season of the female is essentially that of the male, although, in practice, the great majority of females come into oestrous over a relatively short period of time coincident with the period of active rut. Outside of the main rutting period a few precocious females may come into season early. A female who fails to become pregnant at the first heat will return to heat later in the season at an approximate interval of 2–4 weeks, depending on both the species and the individual. The female is capable of returning to heat several times and even to continue heat cycles for several months. Occasionally, a pregnant female will show slight signs of a false heat but will rarely stand for service. In practice, cycling females are extremely rare. The males are extremely efficient at locating and serving oestrous females and probably only 5% of females come into oestrus for a second time and only 1% for a third time. Persistent return to oestrous probably indicates that all is not quite well, although which particular part of a very complex process is malfunctioning is impossible to establish, except perhaps by autopsy. On the other hand, in a young female approaching pregnancy for the first time, a certain amount of running in may well be necessary in some cases, especially those with an internal rather than external control of the cycle. Of the many hundreds of Fallow, Red, Roe, Chinese Water deer, Sika deer, etc., that I have examined at post mortem

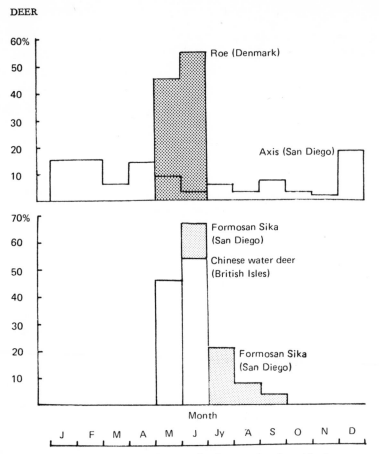

Fig. 9.7 Examples of the main reproductive patterns found in deer as indicated by the time of year at which the young are born.

I have not found any great indication that such false runs were necessary in these seasonal breeders although evidence for silent heats (i.e. oestrous without ovulation) has been found in the ovaries of Red deer and Black Tailed deer on histological examination. By contrast, I have examined a number of female Muntjac at or about puberty and one healthy female had ovulated four times without becoming pregnant and there appeared to be nothing wrong with her reproductive organs. This animal lived wild in a wood with plenty of other male and female Muntjac so had had, on the face of it, ample opportunity to become pregnant.

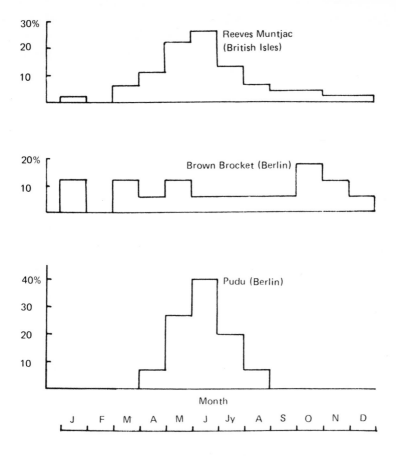

These deer, however, appear to have their reproductive activity largely, if not entirely, under endogenous control and it may simply have been a case of getting everything working in proper synchrony.

The majority of the temperate deer are seasonal breeders and conform to the pattern and seasonal timing of the male as described above. Likewise, those associated with males that are fertile the year round tend towards an apparent aseasonal breeding pattern. Things are not, however, anything like as simple as may at first seem. Muntjac deer are the most enigmatic of this group. Those in the British Isles apparently show a seasonal tendency in births. This can be seen in Fig. 9.7 which collects together data from observed births in Zoos, in the wild and calculated from foetal dimensions. There is little doubt that in all the major populations of the British Isles, the breeding season of the Reeve's Muntjac as evidenced by all the available relevant data is correctly described as a diffuse seasonal pattern as compared with the strongly seasonal pattern in species such as Roe, Red, Pere David's, Pudu, Fallow and Chinese Water deer. Yet, both in the wild and in captivity, my own breeding experiments, and those of my collaborators plus laboratory data establish beyond any doubt that Muntjac can, and frequently do, breed continuously. By this I mean that within a few days of giving birth, the female is again in season and readily accepts service by a male and may normally become pregnant again while she continues to suckle the fawn. The gestation period is about 206 days. Therefore, a sustained breeding pattern of this kind should result in a distribution of births spread evenly through the year unless some highly selective force acts against this. Such a factor had not appeared despite a most careful analysis by several workers. Less strange perhaps, is the fact that after breeding in this fashion for several generations a female may regularly exhibit heats after giving birth but not conceive until several months later. Others may suddenly stop breeding for a long period and not even come into season, only to begin again later. I have ceased to be surprised by anything about the little Muntjac deer. They are very enigmatic and I feel the more one studies them at the moment, the less one is able to explain. It is much safer just to describe rather than interpret! The Brown Brocket breeds throughout the year and births are recorded in most months. Unfortunately, there are too few to establish whether there is any specially favoured time of year. If the fawn is stillborn or dies soon after birth the female mates shortly afterwards. If, however, the fawn survives it is suckled for about $2\frac{1}{2}$ months and the mother will only mate again towards the end of lactation. Thus the interval between successful births is about nine months compared with a gestation period of around 206 days.

True, even year-round breeding does not seem to be a characteristic of any of the Cervidae and this is not entirely surprising. There are probably very few habitats which do not contain some seasonal factor more or less favourable as a period in which to give birth and there is thus evolutionary pressure in favour of birth at such times. In the Axis for example births occur in all months of the year but there are two peaks as seen in Fig. 9.8.

The most accurate knowledge of month of birth usually comes from zoo records and since the circumstances of life in a zoo often differ markedly from the wild, such records need to be treated with caution. The most common error is to assume that a few exceptional breeding records early or late are a part of the normal pattern and to extend the breeding period accordingly. Exceptional records like that are usually an artefact of the zoo situation. Far too much attention is often paid to the abnormal or unusual at the expense of observation or record of the majority and normal pattern.

Environmental Influences on Fertility

Whilst pregnancy is a normal function of the female deer for 7–8 months of the year, it is also a period of stress in which heavy demands will be made on the mother by the foetus at a time when food supplies are restricted and environmental conditions may be at their hardest. Pregnancy is not undertaken lightly, and internal physiological mechanisms set limits in terms of bodily condition to the fecundity of a female in any one year or even whether she will breed at all that year. Females are not physically fully mature in species such as the Red deer until an age of 4–6 years and a similar age applies to other medium to large species. The majority of growth may be achieved by the end of the third year or even less (it depends on both the species and the habitat), but physical development of the female may well be impaired by pregnancy since the foetus has a priority on circulating nutrients and on reserves that the mother may mobilise. Little growth is normally made by the female over the winter period when nutrition is at a level more appropriate to maintenance than growth but a young growing female in the preceding summer and autumn will have been using most of the food for growth rather than building up extensive reserves, although in optimum conditions it might manage both. These problems, however, are clearly exemplified in two parameters of reproduction and the manager will ignore these at his peril. These are the age at puberty and the percentage of early maturing animals, and the index of fecundity with age. The latter, in deer capable of having more than one young, is the average number of young per doe in each age cohort, or simply the pregnancy rate in each cohort in deer having a single young. Examples of different species will illustrate this point.

The European Red deer is found in forests across Europe, in deer parks and in low grade range conditions on the Scottish hills. Each of these range of habitats has its own characteristics. Optimum conditions can be assured in the intensively managed park environment and these animals to some extent must represent the potential of the species as a whole. In these parks, yearling females almost without exception become pregnant but the species has normally only a single young and this is not increased by environmental factors. In the relatively impoverished conditions of the main Scottish Highland deer forests the animals are smaller and there is a considerable range of age at first pregnancy (Mitchell, 1970). About 20% become pregnant as yearlings, most the next year ($2\frac{1}{3}$) and the balance the following year ($3\frac{1}{3}$). In the park animals, the majority of females become pregnant every year but in the Highlands approximately 40% of the adult females may not be pregnant in any one year (Fig 9.8). These are resting and are usually known as yeld hinds and these will normally breed the next season. In this context it is important to distinguish yeld hinds (literally dry, non-milking) that are dry because of a perinatal loss of the fawn and those that did not calve because they were barren that season or were too young.

In the British Isles, the Fallow deer does not appear to experience environmental checks on its reproductive rate, at least in the wild. The great majority of both wild populations and well managed park herds experience puberty at about 16 months and produce a single young each year. Barren females are very few and far between. In some parks, however, there are too many deer and this is reflected in their general appearance and condition. Such situations are normally exceptional and temporary, so that

16   Roe deer male in winter, showing antlers in velvet.

17   Axis (Chital) stag and hinds.

18 Adult female Southern Pudu deer, with juvenile and fawn.

19 Pere David's calf, a few days old.

20 Young Reeves Muntjac buck in summer coat, growing antlers.

21 Mexican Red Brocket deer.

22   Yearling male Mule deer.

23   Red deer stag covering antlers with mud from a wallow.

24 Fallow deer bucks and does during the autumn rut.

25 Canadian bull Moose.

26　Chinese Water deer 'Pippa' giving birth. The first born is sucking and being groomed. The tips of the hooves of the second fawn are visible.

27　. . . . . the second fawn being born . . . . .

28 ..... the second fawn being cleaned .....

29 ..... 'Pippa' eating the placenta while both fawns are sleeping close by.

30 Adult male Southern Pudu deer showing antlers.

31 Reeves Muntjac deer in dense scrub woodland habitat.

32 Chinese Water deer fawn about two weeks old, showing concealment behaviour of older fawns and the lack of ground cover.

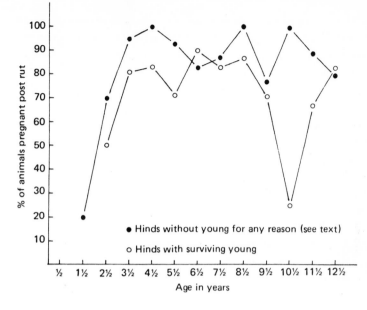

Fig. 9.8 Fertility level of Red deer hinds in Scotland in relation to age and history of previous pregnancy. (Data from Mitchell, 1970.)

I have not been able to follow a heavily overstocked population to assess how the controls did operate. Yet from the examination of the animals shot to reduce the population, it was clear that only about 75% of the animals were carrying foetuses, that the average fawning date that year was later and that at birth the females were in very poor physical condition. The situation would persist far longer than usual as the growth of grass was being taken up by the deer rather than grass growth rapidly entering the stage of excess over consumption. This would exert its own influence on both the nutrition of the young and probably their survival rate and the breeding ability and timing of oestrous in the ensuing rut. It is in conditions like this that the advantage to the individual of puberty after two summers (at 16 months) rather than potentially 4–6 months is appreciated.

In the White Tailed deer there is a potential for up to three young and for puberty in the first year. Leaving aside the affect of age on fecundity it is interesting to see how environmental range conditions affect the age of puberty. In a ten-year period 1939–49 data was obtained by Cheatum and Severinghaus (1950) on fertility among 346 fawns in New York State. Seventy-five of these had become pregnant as fawns at 6–8 months of age. In detail, however, the incidence of fawn breeding was very low in the Adirondack region (about 4%) and much higher (around 32%) in western New York State. The latter deer range was rated as the highest quality range in the State and was heavily hunted, which would suggest a greater and probably higher quality food supply than elsewhere. The influence of the plane of nutrition on puberty and fecundity in the White Tailed deer has also been studied under controlled conditions by Verme. A group of young and prime aged animals were placed in two groups and one was given a low plane diet, the other a high plane. Only seven of the thirteen young animals on the low plane diet were mated and these produced a total of eight fawns. The young animals on the high plane diet of which there were eight, were all mated and these gave birth to a total of thirteen animals. In the latter births, there were five sets of twins and three singletons, whereas there was only one set of twins and six singletons in the low plane group. Thus, the plane of nutrition affected not only the age at breeding but also the fecundity of the fawns.

Moose (*Alces*) also show variations in the percentage of yearlings which become pregnant in different habitats. Markgren (1964) found that about 50% of animals from the coastal area of the Gävleborg county of Sweden had ovulated during October whereas inland it appears that the ovulation rate is lower in this age class. In Newfoundland Moose, Pimlott (1959) found that approximately 60% of females came into breeding condition as yearlings.

The percentage of early breeders also varies as one might expect not only from area to area but also with year. Thus, over a seven-year period the pregnancy rate in yearling Elk (*Cervus*) in the northern Yellowstone herd varied between 0% and 34% with a seven-year mean of 15%. The variation was associated with the severity of winter conditions so that high percentages are correlated with a preceding mild winter rather than with a reduced population density.

The Effect of Age on Fertility

At puberty the female may not always achieve her full reproductive potential. In species with multiple young, aside from any year to year variation in fecundity associated with environmental factors, there may be a period of maturity in which on average the reproductive performance is at a higher level than before or after. It is not always possible to recognise this age related element except in very large samples gathered over many years. This is because the mature cohort of the population is always small in comparison to the numbers of younger animals and a long run of sampling is necessary to balance out the environmental factor. Table 9.1 referring to the work of Cheatum and Severinghaus (1950) is reproduced here in full from Taylor (1956) as it well illustrates these and other points that will be developed later. This table is derived from the examination of hunters' kills

Table 9.1   The Effect of Age on Fertility and the Predicted Contribution of Each Age Cohort to the Total of Births in White Tailed Deer (1948 and 1950 Deer Seasons)*

Age class		Number of animals	Average number of fawns per doe	Predicted births† (rounded)	Percentage of total births
Fawns	$\frac{1}{2}$	944	0·32	302	9
	$1\frac{1}{2}$	915	1·54	1409	42
	$2\frac{1}{2}$	433	1·57	680	20
	$3\frac{1}{2}$	245	1·65	404	12
	$4\frac{1}{2}$	115	2·00	230	6·8
	$5\frac{1}{2}$	75	2·00	150	4·4
	$6\frac{1}{2}$	39	2·00	78	2·3
	$7\frac{1}{2}$	30	2·00	60	1·8
	$8\frac{1}{2}$	20	1·22	24	0·7
	$9\frac{1}{2}$	11	1·22	13	0·4
	$10\frac{1}{2}$	4	1·00	4	0·1
Total		2831		3355	

* Data from Cheatum and Severinghaus, 1950.
† Predicted births = No. animals × average number of fawns per doe.

at roadside checking stations during the 1948 and 1950 antlerless deer season on the western New York State deer range. This is considered to be the highest quality deer range in the State and this, combined with the large sample, is enough to reveal the effect of age on fecundity. From this data has been calculated the fawn crop that would have resulted from these animals. In the first three years of normal reproductive life from $1\frac{1}{2}$–$3\frac{1}{2}$ years, the average number of foetuses is about 1·6 per doe, peak production at around 2 per doe is reached in middle age and thereafter there is a marked drop to around 1·2 per doe. In Roe deer in the British Isles, the writer was unable to isolate from other factors an age related effect on the fecundity of the Roe. In that study the frequency of single and multiple corpora lutea was compared between a sample of 55 yearlings and 76 adults killed over several seasons in five populations in England and Southern Scotland. The frequency of multiple *corpora lutea* was 73% in both yearlings and adults. In this sample only 35 of the animals had foetuses present and again the frequency of twin foetuses in the two age groups 72% and 75% respectively is essentially the same. Roe deer are physically mature much earlier than White Tailed deer and it seems likely that variation in the fertility rate with age is not a characteristic of Roe deer.

The Chinese Water deer is one of the fastest maturing of the deer with only a small increase in weight in the second year of life, in the female around 20% of live weight. This is the most prolific of the deer with from 1–7 foetuses having been recorded in pregnant animals. The average number of foetuses is, however, 2·3 per pregnancy, the highest recorded average for any species of deer. That figure was based on 95 pregnancies and to date the age of the mother has only been confirmed in 24 of these of which only 20 contained visible foetuses. There is no significant change in fecundity with age in that sample, the average number of foetuses being 2·4 in fawns and 2·2 in adults.

There is no evidence that in animals with a single young that age alone is a significant factor affecting fertility. In large series of wild and park Fallow deer, very few animals were found to be not pregnant in normal circumstances. The few that were not pregnant did not indicate that this was in any way related to age and rather

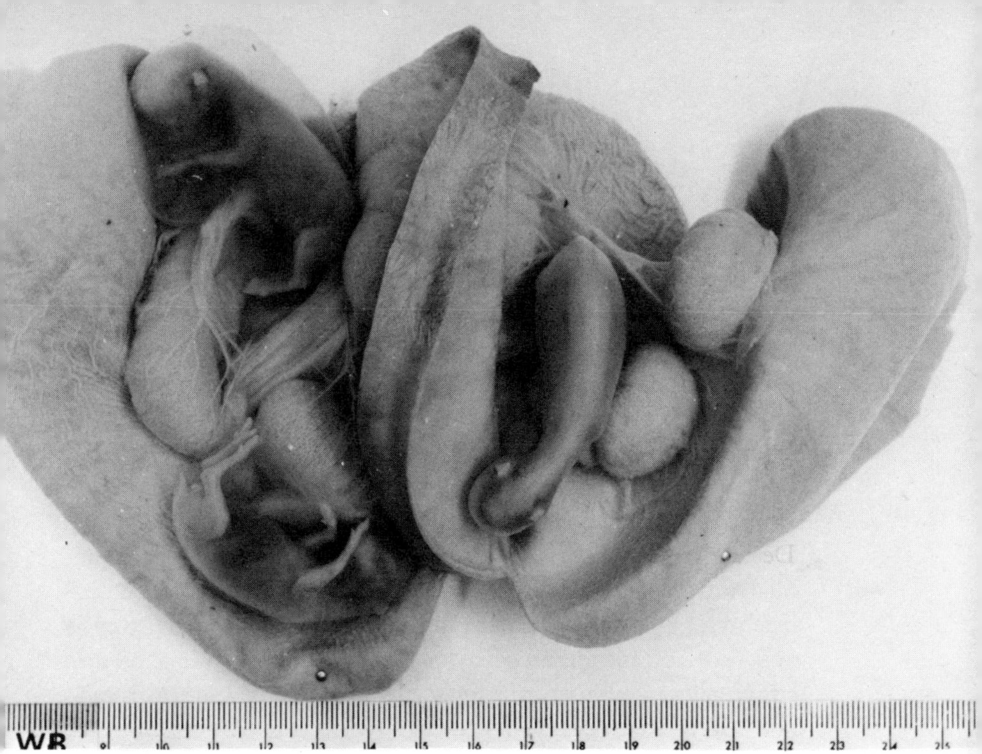

Fig. 9.9 Multiple births are the rule in the Chinese Water deer. Here three foetuses are present in the uterus of a female killed at about the start of the second trimester of pregnancy. The uterus has been opened and the outer fluid-filled sacs have been opened and drained. Each foetus is enclosed within a smaller fluid-filled sac—the amnion. The large nodules are the cotyledonry placenta and the connection of the foetus by the umbilical vessels to this exchange structure is clearly seen. Each cotyledon is a complex interdigitation of maternal and foetal tissues which enables nutrients and gases to be passed to the foetus and waste products removed.

appeared to be an individual circumstance. It would appear that in the wild and in well-managed park herds that females continue to breed throughout their lives on an annual basis.

In the Red deer productivity is seen to fluctuate slightly with age, but this relates to conditions in the Scottish hills where the environment is such that it is necessary for females to miss a pregnancy every few years. Here, an apparent age-related effect is causally related not to age *per se* but to the history of previous pregnancies. This variation does not occur in well managed park herds to anything like the same degree, if indeed it arises at all.

147

The Number of Young

Deer are not prolific breeders as are pigs, for example, and the majority of species produce but a single young in the course of the year. These deer are termed monotoccous, in contrast to those that have more than one young which are termed polytoccous. Environmental factors do influence the number of young in polytoccous species but the others are not normally capable of increasing the number of young in response to environmental factors. The only way that they normally depart from a single young is when the fertilised egg divides to give identical twins. It is theoretically possible that two eggs might ripen simultaneously in the ovary and give rise to non-identical twins. The incidence of twinning in monotoccous deer like Fallow and Red is very low, of the order of 0·001%. In these deer the uterus is structurally capable of carrying twins with one developed in each horn as in Roe deer twins. Pere David's and Reeves Muntjac deer, however, are probably physically incapable of carrying more than one foetus in a normal situation. In these two species, only the right side of the uterus is developed, the left horn even in the foetus is much smaller than the right and in the adult does not develop to any significant extent, so that it would be impossible for a foetus to establish an adequate placental connection and develop in that side. Curiously, the corresponding ovary is unaffected and is as active as the right.

Because environment influences the number of young produced in any one year it is necessary to look at large samples from a variety of populations over several years in order to assess the frequency of the different numbers of young and to gain an idea of the potential productivity of a species. White Tailed deer may have one, two or three young as can the Roe deer. In both species there is the odd report of four foetuses but these are so rare as to be of no importance. Moose (*Alces*) regularly produce twins but most other species do not normally have more than one except for the Chinese Water deer whose weight may double during pregnancy. There is a single report of seven foetuses in the uterus, there are three fully authenticated records of six healthy foetuses in the uterus of animals examined at Woburn. In my studies there the largest number of foetuses in a uterus was four. Several animals had this number and all were healthy. Live litters of four were also found on several occasions.

In all species, the frequency of the different numbers varies from time to time and place to place.

Using the very large sample of White Tailed deer available from different quality ranges, the effect of range quality on fertility in the adults can be measured. It is not easy to quantify range quality but it can, nevertheless, be assessed and roughly graded by those experienced in its management. Such assessments do not imply that every animal on it had the same nutritional status, In fact, this is very definitely not the case for conditions and individual behaviour vary in different parts of that range. However, these huge range areas can be averaged and if the sample of animals from them is similarly large to balance out the effects of extremes then valid inter-area comparisons can be made. In the New York State survey of White Tailed deer on five ranges the highest levels of fertility were found in the western range (1·71 per doe) and the lowest (1·06 per doe) in the Central Adirondack range estimated to be the poorest of the five (Cheatum and Severinghaus, 1950). Other ranges had intermediate values. There are data to indicate that when range conditions are improved in terms of food supply either by cropping down the herd or increasing food availability by felling timber, that increased fecundity rates result. The difficulty of interpreting these data is always the problem of isolating each possible factor the way it can be done in laboratory experiments with, say, mice. You simply cannot do this in wildlife management experiments and they, therefore, need to be planned, executed and analysed with very great care, and with built in controls. It seems so obvious that nutrition should affect productivity that we tend to take it for granted that it does so. In fact, the controls may be much more subtle and we may not be isolating the responsible factor—the ultimate factor—at all. As long as management operations achieve the desired result, there is little tendency to question the assumptions. We should, however, because there will be a time when things do not work or we may be dealing with a species or situation where there is no margin for error.

With the British Roe deer studies the individual populations are so small and the area generally so diversified as to make it impractical to classify individual populations in terms of range quality. Most ranges appear to support the deer at a reasonable level and in most cases migration would appear to be a feasible alternative to restricted feeding. On a national basis, there are three broad groups of Roe habitat. In southern England, conditions are generally milder and the temperature warmer than further north. This is reflected in longer growing seasons. Woodlands are invariably small and are regularly scattered amongst arable and grass fields providing the deer with a considerable variety of food. In northern England and southern Scotland, the growing season is somewhat shorter. Most woodlands are at higher elevations and the majority of these are softwood plantations. Blocks of woodland are generally larger than in the south and the surroundings are more often permanent grassland than arable crops. Further north, the Roe populations in the present Roe study were all from large softwood forests generally on upland areas surrounded by rough grazing. On this general basis, the populations theoretically occupied habitats which were relatively poorer in the north than either the central or southern areas. Within these divisions there were, however, populations at varying densities which would affect the quantity of food available and also woodlands at various stages of development which affected the quantity and variety of forage. None of these variables could be quantified to arrive at an index of nutritional quality. Overstocking is not a matter of numbers alone but of numbers in relation to available food. For this reason, despite detailed studies of each population involved in the survey, for the final analysis the data was pooled on the regional basis described above.

The animals studied in the survey were killed in normal management operations by forestry and management staff between October and March some 3–8 months after the rut. Thus, all information relates to the animal at the time of death and not at the time of mating. It is, in fact, the situation at and around mating that really concerns us but we cannot by any acceptable means study this. Because the Roe deer blastocyst lies dormant until the New Year (see Chapter 13 below) there is no significant strain on the mother

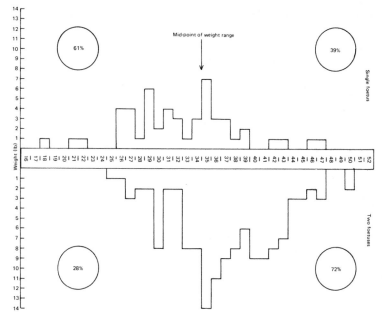

Fig. 9.10   The relationship between body weight and fecundity in Roe deer from England and Scotland.

in terms of nutrition in the period during which the deer were shot, nor in most forests has there been much significant restriction of food supply by this time. Condition of the mother might, therefore, relate to the general condition earlier in the year. If body weight is used as an index of condition or of the general quality of the range, fecundity can be compared in animals of different weight. Fig. 9.10 shows the weights of Roe deer in different populations against which is plotted the occurrence of single or multiple *corpora lutea* in the ovaries (for practical purposes at this point these correspond with the number of foetuses). In the heaviest half of the sample 72% of the animals had multiple *corpora lutea* and 39% only one, whereas in the lower half of the weight range only 28% had multiples and 61% a single *corpus luteum*. Thus, the heavier carcasses in winter-killed animals are associated with animals having the highest fecundity levels. If the tentative correlation between condition at breeding and winter weight is accepted then size which relates to feeding conditions suggests a correlation between nutritional levels and fecundity in the Roe.

On the basis of the relative feeding quality of the three main Roe deer regions in the British Isles it is to be expected that an adequate sample from these regions would show some variation in fecundity between the regions. If the data for the nine-year period are collated on a regional basis, it is found that the frequency of multiple *corpora lutea* and multiple foetuses declines from south to north. In the north, the frequency of multiple *corpora lutea* is 63% and of foetuses 42% compared with 83% and 72% in the south.

For the monitoring of breeding performance biologists and managers have established simple basic items which they record. In animals killed the weight and the age of the animal are compared with information from the ovaries indicating the number of eggs ovulated, or the lack of ovulation, and the number, size and sex of any foetuses visible in the uterus. Such data is obtained from culled animals or casualties. These data have an objective value and are part of a continuous monitoring record and have considerable predictive value for the year ahead. Live deer are monitored in terms of total populations, dispersions and the birth and survival rate of the young. At all stages of the reproductive cycle there is a tendency to diminish the number of young, and how and why this occurs is important.

The number of eggs produced at ovulation is indicated by the number of corpora lutea in the ovaries. Each *corpus luteum* forms from a single follicle after this has ruptured and the egg has left the follicle to enter the fallopian tube. In monotoccous species, only one follicle is usually ruptured at each oestrous and the timing of ovulation is carefully synchronised with many other physiological activities necessary for mating and pregnancy. In polytoccous species, several follicles may rupture at or about the same time and their closeness in time may well determine the fate of the eggs. It was thought for a long time that only a single egg was present in each follicle. Any twins from a single ovulation would always be of the same sex since these could only result from the division of the egg in the fallopian tubes. However, it has been found by the writer in Roe deer and by Pimlott in Elk that there are in these species follicles which contain two egg cells, as different sex twins have been found in the uterus associated with ovulation from only one follicle. The frequency of these follicles is low in Roe, perhaps about 2%, and possibly less in Elk (*Alces*).

The egg is fertilised from the male's spermatozoa which have worked their way from the cervix through the chambers of the uterus and up the fallopian tubes. Fertilisation occurs in the tube and the egg migrates down the tube, the cells dividing and multiplying as it goes. At the same time hormones are at work preparing the uterus to receive the egg which is now at the stage of development known as a blastocyst.

Once in the uterus the blastocyst begins to elongate, the membranes develop and attach themselves to the special plaques on the wall of the uterus forming a placenta. Up to this point there is the greatest chance of the pregnancy failing in whole or part. Because of the rapid changes in the chemical secretions of the uterus and tubes any eggs entering them at the wrong stage will probably die. This would be the case where there are two eggs ovulated from different follicles in either ovary but the time interval between them is too great. We do not know how close together ovulations must occur for both to survive. The fertilisation of the first egg ensures that conditions will be wrong for the second.

Mating is normally effective. If at least one egg is not fertilised the whole cycle of ovulation begins again and the female returns to oestrous 2–4 weeks later. Something like 95% of animals become pregnant at the first ovulation. The relative loss of young between ovulation and implantation (the period of active initial formation of the placenta which occurs when the embryo is 2–3 cm (0·8–1·2 in) long) can be determined by comparison of the number of *corpora lutea* with the number of foetuses present. Animals that have recently ovulated in which the embryo is too small to be detected yet must be ignored.

In the Roe deer in animals having only one *corpus luteum* the number of foetuses slightly exceeded the number of *corpora lutea* (ratio 1·09) because of identical twinning and polyovular follicles.

Of 229 animals with two *corpora lutea* 45 (ratio 0·91) had only a single foetus indicating a partial failure of 20% of potential twin pregnancies. The precise cause of these losses cannot be established with certainty but since such high rates are associated only with those ovulating from two follicles there would seem to be a link. This is supported by the even greater mortality of ova found when three follicles ovulate (ratio 0·70). The same is seen in the Chinese Water deer Table 9.2, the greater the number of ova per ovulation the greater the mortality. It may, therefore, be as suggested above, that unless these ovulations are very close, that conditions may change and adversely affect the ova from later ovulations. Clearly, the more follicles involved the greater the difficulty of ensuring that these rupture nearly together. Despite this, a great many are successful. This alone is unlikely to account for all the pre-implantation mortality, as some ova may be defective and others may fail to become fertilised at all.

Mortality of embryos and foetuses (as they are later called) is very small in all the species that I have studied and on which there is any body of data. In the Roe deer and White Tailed deer, both twins and triplets manage to obtain an adequate area of placental attachment and it is very unusual to find any significant difference in weight between the foetuses attributable to restricted food supply. In Chinese Water deer conditions can become very crowded and I have seen one animal in which there was a dead embryo along with three larger healthy foetuses and one preg-

Table 9.2 Relationship Between the Ovulation Rate and Implantation Rate in Chinese Water Deer

Number of *corpora lutea*	Number of animals	Implantation rate (%)*
1	6	100·0
2	30	98·6
3	25	85·1
4–6	8	77·8

$$* \quad \frac{\text{Number of foetuses}}{\text{Number of } corpora\ lutea} \times \frac{100}{1}$$

nancy where one foetus with a rather limited placental attachment was alive but only about half the size of the others.

A number of deer of all species may not be pregnant because the uterus is occupied by a dead foetus that has been retained long after death. In such cases it is not easy to determine when death occurred or why the foetus was not expelled. The remains of the foetus have become impacted in the shrunken uterus (Fig. 11.1) and in most cases have either become mummified or are putrid. In such cases, death could well result from toxaemia but has not done so. Whether such foetuses are ultimately expelled I do not know and if they were it is not known whether a further pregnancy would be possible. One unusual pregnancy that could only have ended fatally was found in a Sika deer. The wall of the uterus had been split some time previous to pregnancy. The foetus had formed a placenta within the uterus but had slipped out through the hole. With further growth it could not get back in and was growing in the abdominal cavity. There is no reason why this animal would not have developed to term but delivery would have been impossible resulting in both the death of the foetus and mother.

The greatest mortality once pregnancy is well established is in the perinatal period. This is associated with a variety of factors and these are considered separately in the following chapters.

10 Life in the Uterus

The first 6–8 months of life of any of the deer will be spent within the mother's uterus. During this time the young will grow from a fluid-filled ball of cells, about as big as a pinhead, to a fully-formed youngster, capable of following its mother within a few hours of birth. At birth it may weigh anything from about 0·4 kg (14 oz) in the smallest species to 10 kg (22 lb) in a Pere David's calf and 14 kg (31 lb) in Wapiti.

A selection of gestation periods are given in Table 10.1, together with the average birth weight of the young. From this data it is possible to construct a graph which will show the weight of the foetus on a given day. The great value of this is that from Fig. 10.2

Table 10.1   Average Gestation periods and Birth Weights of Some Deer Species

Species	Average gestation period (days)	Average birth weight (kg)
Chinese Water deer	176	0·8
Reeve's Muntjac	210	1·0
White Tailed deer	200	3.0
Southern Pudu	c. 212	0·4
Brown Brocket	206	1·3
Fallow deer	230	4.5
Red (Rhum)	230	6·5
Roe (Nb delayed implantation)	(149 + 145)*	2·0
Pere David's	c. 280	9·4
Japanese Sika	217	2·7–3·6

* See Chapter 13.

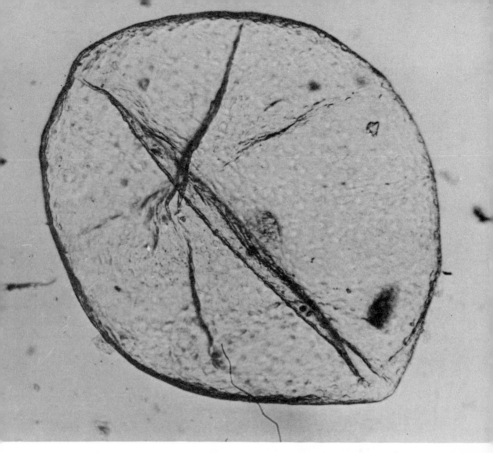

Fig. 10.1 Photomicrograph of the blastocyst of a Muntjac deer. The blastocyst is a tiny fluid-filled ball of cells and is the stage at which the conceptus enters the uterus. This blastocyst, which has collapsed somewhat during preservation, was 4 mm across.

the date of conception and the date of birth of the foetus can be calculated within approximate limits. The graph is not reliable at the beginning nor at the end of pregnancy because of the nature of foetal development at such times, but in between it can be most useful in estimating the age of foetuses.

The fertilised egg enters the uterus as a spherical ball of cells up to about 5 mm in diameter and filled with fluid. It looks just like a miniature football. Visible as a mark on the surface are the cells which will develop into the embryo, the rest will form the membranes.

For the first three weeks or so there will be no functional con-

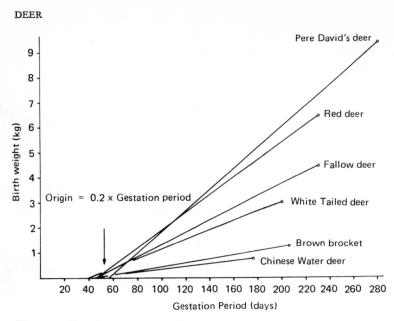

Fig. 10.2 Foetal growth rates of deer.

nection between the mother and the embryo. During this time, the embryo will be nourished from its own food reserves and by the absorption of the secretions of the uterus. Waste products diffuse into the fluid centre of the blastocyst. In its development, the blastocyst will begin to elongate into a sac which will penetrate into both horns of the uterus right to their tips. In fact, there are three membranous, tough, elastic sacs involved. The embryo is entirely contained within a fluid-filled sac, the amnion. Totally enclosing the amnion, and thus the embryo, is another large sac, the chorion. Occupying the space between the amnion and the chorion is a fluid filled sac—the allantois—which keeps the chorion fully distended and thereby also the uterus. On opening a uterus, the distinction between chorion and allantois is not immediately apparent, but puncturing the sac and allowing the fluid to gush out reveals that the two sacs were in contact with each other—so that it is difficult to separate the chorion without puncturing the inner allantois. After emptying the allantois, the much smaller fluid-filled amniotic sac is seen surrounding the

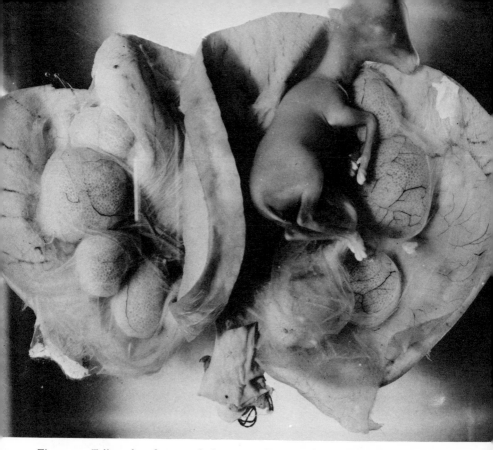

Fig. 10.3   Fallow deer foetus and placenta at the start of the second trimester of pregnancy. The uterus and the enclosing membranes have been opened to show the nature of the cotyledonry placenta. The placenta which is the means of exchange of essential nutrients and gases and the removal of waste products between the mother and foetus consists of a complex interdigitation of foetal and maternal tissues. In deer, unlike humans, the placenta comprises a number of discrete elements called cotyledons—each a mini-placenta—these are the spherical cellular looking bodies eight of which can be seen in the photograph. A single foetus is the rule in Fallow deer, but irrespective of which side of the uterus the foetus is in, the cotyledons develop in both. This is not always the case in other species.

foetus. Its fluid is self-contained and has no connection with that from the allantois.

The amniotic fluid provides the environment necessary for the development of all land mammals and protects the foetus from injury. The allantois is concerned with the nutrition, respiration and excretion of the foetus, whilst the chorion provides the physical connection between mother and foetus.

When the embryo is small, about 1–2 cm (0·4–0·8 in) long, the sac usually fills both of the horns and at this time can be gently separated from the uterus and lifted out. On examination, it will be seen that there are oval areas with numerous raised pimple-like structure (called villi) on the surface of the chorion. These are the cotyledonary plaques which are developed opposite to, and correspond with, raised areas of the uterine wall, called caruncles. The cotyledonary villi and the maternal caruncles are the two structures —one foetal, the other maternal—which will together form the placenta. The placenta is essentially a structure composed of maternal and foetal cells, which allows the mother to nourish the foetus and remove the waste products of metabolic activity. The structure of the placenta varies a great deal between species. That of the deer is similar to the cow. There is not a single sheet of tissue, as in humans, but instead a number of separate, smaller placentae known as cotyledons. The number varies as does their size and distribution between the horns of the uterus, but that is a matter of individual variation and has no functional significance.

Fig. 10.4 (*opposite*) Electron micrograph ($\times 4350$) of a minute portion of the placenta of a Muntjac deer. Finger-like processes (villi) of foetal tissues lie in deep crypts formed in the maternal tissues. There are many thousands of these in the placenta as a whole. The surface of each villus is covered by a single layer of columnar cells of foetal origin whilst the crypt is lined by a similar layer of cuboidal-shaped cells of maternal origin. At their free surface, these cells are in intimate contact and microvilli from both sides interdigitate, creating a very large surface area of contact so that substances can be exchanged between the foetal and maternal cells. The substances to be exchanged are transported from the base of the cells, where they enter or leave the capillary network. Beneath both the maternal and foetal epithelia there is a layer of connective tissue cells which provide support for the structure and contain the capillaries etc. This micrograph shows portions of a few of these cells magnified to a degree where the constituents and organelles of the individual cells are clearly seen. The whole being a cross section of the functional region of an active placenta. The major structures are identified as follows. MS in the top left hand corner is the only portion of the maternal connective tissue septum to be seen. ME indicates the band of maternal epithelial cells whose microvilli (MV) interdigitate with those of the foetal Epithelial cells (FE) at whose base is seen part of a capillary (FC) which lies amongst the connective tissue of the foetal villus.

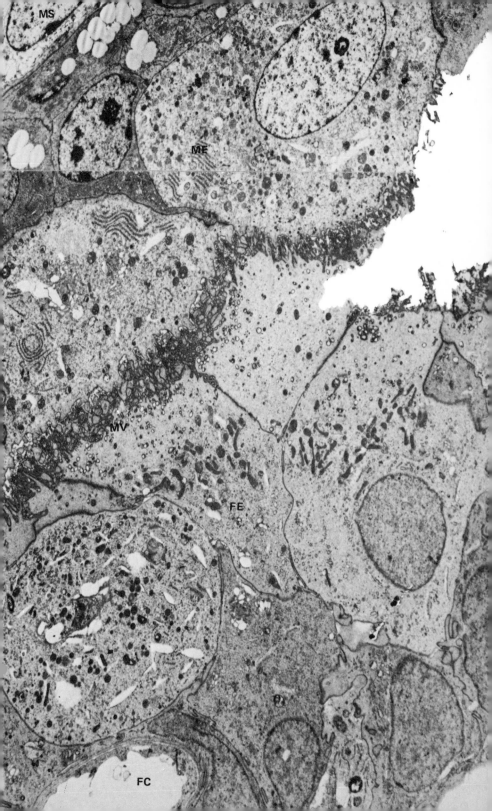

In the fallow deer, the average number of cotyledons is about ten. Each cotyledon forms as the result of the interaction between the villous plaques on the chorion, and the crypts which will form on the caruncles opposite to the villi. Effectively, the villi of the foetus invade the crypts, developing in the caruncle. The whole structure develops and increases in size and complexity during pregnancy, so that the final arrangement comes to resemble a forest of dendritic villi surrounded by maternal tissue. Foetal cells abut maternal cells. At their bases are the whole network of blood vessels which transport the solid and gaseous materials to and from the cells effecting the exchange. Under the electron microscope can be seen the nature of this arrangement and at the highest magnifications the tiny packages of substances are seen being transported across. The workings of these structures are shown and explained in the captions to the accompanying illustrations.

As the foetus grows so do the placenta, membranes and uterus. The amount of body tissue and fluid involved is very considerable and in the case of the Chinese Water deer, the mother may double her non-pregnant weight. All the nourishment for this must come from the mother's body either from the food being consumed or from the reserves stored in the body. The foetus has a priority over the majority of other bodily functions of the mother in terms of the food available. It is for this reason that late summer conditions and the careful synchrony of fawning with the new growth of plants is of such vital importance.

The foetus is clearly recognisable as a deer from quite early on. Absolute sizes vary, of course, between the species; but in the Roe deer, for example, most of the structures of the adult deer are already present when the foetus is 3–4 cm long and it can now be sexed. At a time about two-thirds of the way through pregnancy, the foetus is fully covered with its hair coat and spots that it will have at birth—and in terms of length, it is fairly close to its size at birth. The foetus has, however, a great deal to accomplish in the final trimester, very little of which is apparent to outside scrutiny. It is for this reason that many animals which are killed are described as having a full term foetus when, in fact, there is a long way still to go. This last phase is concerned with the maturation of the individual organs and the general filling out of the body. Hence, continued development is best indicated by the increasing weight of the foetus, rather than its length. There is, however, quite a lot of variation in weight at birth, much of it due to the nutritional state of the mother. The young mature rapidly in the last few days and when everything is ready (we do not know how this is determined) the young are born. This rapid maturation of key organs such as the lungs is a feature of the last few days and without this development the young can only survive a few hours if born or delivered prematurely. Whether such fawns could live if given the intensive care treatment of the human baby, I am not sure. Far better to leave all to the mother.

11 *Birth and Beyond*

Because of the animal's way of life, very few people have observed and recorded the birth of a deer and the subsequent development of the young. These are, however, vital stages in the life cycle and what happens in those first few hours is crucial. The study of the birth and the behaviour of the mother and young then, and as they develop, is of considerable interest in its own right and also of much wider relevance. The science of animal behaviour is relatively young and many of the studies on deer are breaking new ground, or extending a very limited field of knowledge. Our observations on the birth and aftercare of the young in deer, both in captivity and in the wild, opened up many new horizons and taught us much that we have been able to apply to other individuals and species. I have been very fortunate in being able to study the reproductive biology of the Chinese Water deer in the field, laboratory and home, and watching, rearing, filming, etc. far more than any other species—and although this deer is perhaps the most unusual of its kind, it is the one that we have the greatest knowledge of and involvement with. Every species of deer is different, so that in this chapter it is necessary to select from the available data, with one species to serve as the main example and to refer to others as necessary. The reader will perhaps excuse my choice, for whilst others have written on this in other species to some extent, the work on the Chinese Water deer has not yet been published and would otherwise be unavailable.

Below is a description and illustration of the births of two deer. Both mothers were a year old and were giving birth for the first time. Each had been hand reared by us and they lived with a male in our garden. The first birth described was to Pippa who was exceedingly tame. The other, Becky, was not and could not for her own sake be approached. Pippa's birth was also filmed.

Becky was the first to give birth but the order here is reversed so that the normal birth to Pippa could be described first:

'At midnight on the 29th of June I examined Pippa and there was no evidence of labour, although from the size of her mammary gland we had judged parturition to be imminent for several days. At this time she was laying with the male Max and both were cudding. This was the normal behaviour at that time of night. She was observed again at 04.15 hours and was still laying with Max. She was in labour. Every few minutes, short bouts of low amplitude contractions passed across her abdomen. Detailed recording was commenced at 04.30 and Max was moved into the lower half of the garden. In the next quarter of an hour she changed places several times and then finally settled on her right side. Throughout these observations I was standing only a few feet from her. At 04.45 the vagina began to open and a fluid-filled sac could be seen inside. A few moments later, a small volume of fluid trickled from the vulva and this was the only loss of fluid seen. Groups of contractile waves across the abdomen were becoming more frequent. They varied from 9 to 18 in a group, at intervals of from a half to four minutes. The contractions were shallow and rapid. She lay on her right side with fore and hind legs outstretched and eyes half-shut. This contrasts with Becky's straining contractions accompanied by body stretching. At 04.55 the sac was showing through the vulva and the tips of the fore feet were visible. At this point Pippa stretched quite a lot, but did not lick herself as Becky had done. The head of the foetus appeared at 05.07 and the rest of the trunk was gradually eased out by gentle straining. The fawn was free and on the ground at 05.12. She licked at the sac once or twice as it came out, licked and looked at it when it was out and then rose. This movement freed the attachments and she then lay down again. Both she and the fawn adjusted their positions slightly and she gently licked it removing traces of the sac and mucous still adhering. The fawn was sucking at the hind teat within ten minutes of birth.

At approximately the same time as sucking commenced a second sac with a single foot in it appeared through the vagina. At this point I inserted my fingers into the vagina and checked the position of the foetus. It lay with its head on outstretched fore feet, with the tip of its nose about two inches from the vulva. This was at 05.25. Little progress was made with the second delivery in the next ten minutes but she then steadily eased the foetus out still laying on her right side. When the foetus was about half-way out and the shoulders were free, she rose and eased it out, the foetus threshing from side to side. The foetus was finally delivered when she was laying on the ground. Once it was out she ignored it, leaving it struggling feebly for several minutes while she continued to lick the first fawn. The second fawn attempted to struggle towards her and we moved it a few inches further, whereupon she immediately started to lick and groom it. The second fawn sucked for the first time at 06.03. The first fawn was on its feet for the first time at 06.05 and the second fawn at 06.30. From then till 07.00, she continued to groom and suckle the fawns though no trace of fluid could be seen coming from the nipples. The fawns sucked all four teats but it was the hind pair that they both sought first.

The fawns began to wander around, attracted by any movement that I made or by the movement of the deer in the lower half of the garden, but at 07.00 they both curled up and went to sleep. At 06.04, further light abdominal quiverings with occasional thrusting was noted at fairly frequent intervals in Pippa. These are thought to have been associated with the expulsion of the placenta for at about 07.15 the placenta was expelled and she spent about half-an-hour pulling pieces of it out and eating them. Unlike Becky she took no other food with it. When the placenta had been eaten, she thoroughly licked herself all over although there was no mess or fluid apparent to us. After this, the fawns woke up and were very active. They frequently sucked and went off on short investigatory trips, returned, slept, sucked again and so on. At about 08.00 Pippa went and ate some leaves and then returned to the fawns licking and sucking them and retrieving them. The fawns slept for most of the morning. When exploring the fawns made a soft drawn-out "Pee-ouw". Pippa was not heard to make any call to them. We identified and measured the fawns at 09.00. The first-born fawn was a female weighing 1·05 kg (2·3 lb) and the second was a male weighing 1·1 kg (2·4 lb).'

These two fawns were the largest fawns that we recorded on day one. Their sense of teat position was extremely good.

On the first morning both fawns were attracted to any large moving object. On the first night there was heavy rain and although we put the fawns under cover several times they immediately got up again to lay out in the open. From about midday on day one it was clear that both fawns had distinct behaviour patterns. One spent a lot of time sleeping; the other liked to explore. During the afternoon each chose where it wanted to lay and stayed separate from the other and Pippa. The same happened during the storm that night although during the rain Pippa went and licked them fairly often. They also got up and shook themselves at intervals in the same way as the adult does. Their coats were extremely waterproof for although the outside was wet and there was rain running from it, it was warm and dry beneath.

On day two, the fawns were only rarely attracted to moving objects and showed a dislike of other animals including humans. On day three, the fawns appeared to have become fully identified with their mother and the other deer as they usually attempted to conceal themselves or to run away when we approached them. This may be influenced by the fact that once a day they were picked up, weighed and measured!

Here now is a description of the birth of twin fawns to Chinese Water deer Becky:

'When first observed at 08.00 hours, she was recumbent on her left side with legs outstretched. She repeatedly stretched her hind-legs and neck, fidgeted and licked her flanks, udder and back. At 09.00 hours, waves of muscular contractions were clearly visible across the abdomen and she would strain for several seconds at a time with hind-legs and neck extended. At about 09.22, there was a slight discharge of fluid from the vagina. At 09.25 she rose and a fluid-filled sac approximately 15 cm (6 in) in diameter was bulging from the vagina. Within this, the forepart of the foetus could be seen. She fidgeted, laying down and getting up, several times in the next few minutes. Whilst laying down, she gave three long thrusts, within half a minute each of which expelled the foetus several centimetres. She then rose and the foetus enclosed in the sac fell clear. As it hit the ground, the foetus was struggling vigorously and she swiftly turned on it, bit through the membranes, and licked the struggling fawn vigorously. She lay down with it and groomed it almost continuously for several minutes, and thereafter with only infrequent pauses. At 10.15 the fawn was on its feet and sucking from Becky, who still lay laterally recumbent on her left side. Its attempts at sucking and teat location were poor and it kept emitting the soft low squeak, which in a fawn is a mild distress call. Grooming and suckling of the fawn continued on and off until 12.30, when we had to intervene. At 09.50, whilst she was grooming the fawn, Becky was also stretching and licking her hind regions and around 10.00 hours was eating some of the umbilicus and membranes taking mouthfuls of grass between. By approximately 11.15, it was clear that she was trying to expel another foetus. By 11.30, its sac filled with yellow fluid had appeared and a slight flow of blood and mucus persisted. A few minutes later, threshing feet appeared in the sac. Although she lay, strained, rose, lay down again several times, no more progress was made with expelling the foetus and several times the sac retracted into the vagina. Throughout this time, she kept licking herself and the sac and several times pulled at it with her teeth to no avail. She also continued to lick her fawn. By 12.15, movement of the foetus had ceased and we went to examine her. At our approach, however, she fled, rupturing the fluid filled sac as she did so. We therefore left her alone. At about 12.30, we observed that she had managed to pull the dead foetus out by its membranes and that it came out hind quarters first. When she had pulled it free and it had fallen to the ground she paid no attention to it at all and returned to look after the live fawn. Between 13.00 and 14.00 hours, she expelled the placenta but did not eat all of it. The next day she found some pieces of the umbilicus on the ground and ate these.'

It would appear that the second foetus would have been born within about half an hour of the first had it not been for the fact that it was malpresented. The malpresentation involved Becky in considerable effort attempting to expel it. Her fidgety behaviour and the distress call of the fawn suggest that the malpresentation adversely affected her care of the firstborn.

From our observations on very young fawns at Whipsnade and Woburn, as well as those in our garden the following general points can be made:

1 For some hours after birth the mother and young stay close together, but after this the mother remains separate from the fawn for many hours at a time;

2 Nursing appears to be infrequent, probably at intervals of six hours or more;

3 The fawns are born one at a time and are groomed before delivery of the next;

4 In multiple births the litter is loosely grouped and contrasts with the arrangement in pigs;

5 Within a variable period, from 6–24 hours after birth, the young fawns may show concealment behaviour, however, this is preceded by a period when the young fawn will be attracted by any large or moving object;

6 This attraction to large or moving objects is seen when the mother is actively displaced from the young whilst carrying out initial nursing. It is possible that in normal circumstances the mother does not leave the young until this phase is over;

7 The mother recognises her fawn by scent. On one occasion when three fawns had been found separately, three mothers were showing interest in them. As each fawn was released each mother would go after it, sniff it, but only one would continue with the fawn. On another occasion, a mother approached a tagged fawn, went up to it, sniffed the tag and shied away and did so repeatedly. By this means she had eventually drawn the fawn about three hundred yards away from where it had been tagged and only then did she suckle it. Throughout this time the fawn had been emitting distress cheeps;

8 Licking of the fawn appears to be important both to the

mother and to the young. For the young it serves to cleanse the coat of the sticky products of birth, which if they are not thoroughly removed, leave the coat matted and the animal vulnerable to wetting. In a properly groomed fawn, in which grooming has lasted for at least thirty minutes, the coat is thoroughly dry, shiny, flat and often feels greasy. It is possible that licking may stimulate secretion from the skin or hair follicles which serve to waterproof it. The drying of the coat also prevents heat loss due to evaporation. The licking appears to comfort the fawn; it also elicits reciprocal licking of the mother by the fawn and may also add a distinctive scent to the fawn, by which the mother is able to identify it.

A dead fawn elicits no maternal response from the mother. On one occasion a litter of triplets was found and the mother accidentally displaced from them. The first two animals were well groomed but the third was not groomed. Although we retreated and the mother returned, when we came back several hours later, the mother had removed the two groomed fawns and left the one that was not groomed. It is therefore possible that licking by the mother is a precondition of her acceptance and recognition of her young.

It would appear from our observations of the reactions of fawns that imprinting and development of the bond between mother and young is largely established in the first day, particularly in the first six hours, when the fawn is first groomed and suckled. After this time the fawn is left while the mother feeds and she returns only to suckle and groom it. It would appear that these early bonds are by no means absolute and require reinforcement over a longer period. Our hand-reared female, Pippa, came from a mother which died in labour. She was brought up later with two other fawns, but in her first few days she was entirely dependent on us for food and succour. Her subsequent companion, Max, was between one and two days old when found and was distrustful of us, although he fed readily. He was always more timid, although relatively tame. The third, Becky, was about three days old when found and was not brought to us until she was about a week old. She was always very wild. A fourth animal, probably ten days old when found, was entirely wild and never became tame.

Identification with the mother appears to be associated with both olfactory, auditory, visual and tactile cues. It is suspected that the main cause of the abandonment of young fawns that have been handled by humans is due to olfactory rejection. This does not seem to occur in the handling of the older animals, and the critical time is probably when these bonds are being developed. The human smell probably masks that of the mother and fawn. The displacement of the mother for any length of time during the first few hours after birth may also result in rejection. It is for these reasons that, as far as possible, we avoid handling young fawns. By taking particular care in handling and tagging them, the death rate amongst tagged fawns is no more than that amongst untagged ones. We avoid displacing mothers from their young whilst they are grooming them.

There is a belief that most deer births occur in the early hours of the morning. There is little body of data about this on any species and such as there is tends to reflect the time over which people are about—08.00–16.00—rather than the twenty-four hours over which deer are active. I have seen births taking place through the day and have found others which indicated birth through the night, though since most births are in May/June, night is rather short if that term refers solely to hours of darkness. I think the consensus of the data available is that deer will give birth at any time of the day and night.

Where deer give birth is another matter. In my studies on the Chinese Water deer I concluded that there was no choice of birth site in regard to cover, shade or any tangible factor. That, of course, referred to the fawns that were found! Perhaps the others were much better hidden. In Roe deer at Cheddington, close observation of the mothers indicated a preparation for birth and the selection some days before of a secluded area. The behaviour of the mother enabled the fawns to be located easily after birth. The term 'easily' is perhaps misleading, as anyone who has looked for fawns will know that hours can be spent in cover looking for a fawn that one knows is there! Fallow deer in parkland mostly give birth in bracken or long grass if this is available. There is no doubt that the Fallow chooses to give birth in ample cover. In the same parks, the Red deer is not so fussy; some will be born in cover, but many more are to be found in areas of rough grassland with little attempt at concealment in vegetation; likewise the Pere David's deer.

The young of deer in their normal habitat are very well camouflaged. The majority are spotted with much paler spots than the ground colour of the back. They are said to resemble the dapples of light coming through the leaves, but I think the spot and stripe patterns are better regarded as a disruptive patterning. To this is added the behavioural aspects of camouflage, the low lying position and the immobility. It is also said that most species of deer have little or no scent. Certainly, trained working dogs are of no help when looking for fawns. There are two positions usually adopted by hiding fawns. In the first, they are curled up as if resting, and the second is stretched out and lying close. I have seen both kinds of behaviour in the same species, and I think that the former is a feature of resting of younger animals and the second is a feature of older and more alert animals that may have dropped into this position for concealment.

I have spoken quite a lot about matters arising from the observation, catching and recording of very young deer as part of a carefully controlled research programme. It would be very wrong, if in addition to what is written below and has been stated above, that I did not in the strongest possible terms warn others: *do not attempt the casual location and handling of young deer.* To do this would involve a great deal of risk of death to young deer and also distress to the population as a whole. There are many tricks involved in this work to avoid such occurrences if the work has to be undertaken, but these cannot be described here. I would add that deer do not make household pets, most fawns picked up as abandoned and taken for rearing do not last 48 hours. The few that do make it usually end up in a zoo pen, having created chaos and injury.

Perinatal Mortality

On the farmland area in the Chinese Water Deer study the perinatal mortality is very high. The terrain here comprised either grazed permanent grassland or young barley and the fawns are born in these fields. In contrast, the woodland study areas had good ground cover and the parkland area contained much rough grass and sedge clumps. Perhaps because of this much greater cover, we found relatively few young, but the number of dead ones was very much less than on the farm. The farm had the greatest density of deer (about 2–3 per acre). On the farm, the mortality occurred in the first three days of life and at the beginning of the fawning season was about 25% of births. As the season progressed and growth of grass and crops increased, it became more difficult to locate fawns. There was no evidence of deaths in fawns more than three days old.

It is not easy to establish the cause of death as within a few minutes the body had been flensed by crows. Despite a careful watch, crows were never observed to attack even a dying fawn. In some cases, two or three dead fawns were found as close to one another as in live litters. The coats had not been groomed. The fact that they were found together, all ungroomed, suggests that they were stillborn, as the mother always cleanses one fawn before the birth of the next. It is probable that the first, and perhaps the others, were malpresented. Prolonged labour also has an adverse effect on the mother's response. Single dead fawns are not so easy to account for as they could be from a single or multiple birth. Some of the singletons were not groomed and were presumably dead at birth through malpresentation. Other fawns are known to have lived for several days after being cleansed. Human disturbance could be responsible but in the particular circumstances of the farm seemed a little unlikely. Added to this are deaths due to specific factors, which can include falling into holes, death of the mother, etc. and in deer in general these hazards will play an important part in perinatal mortality.

The majority of the deaths of fawns apparently receiving maternal attention are thought to be due to environmental factors. The majority of the fawns are born on open ground with little or no cover and their coats are dark. In the two years over which this mortality was first recorded, it was extremely hot, with day after day of strong sunshine. Many of the fawns, when found, were panting. Their small size and infrequent suckling by the mother could well result in overheating and dehydration, which could directly or indirectly lead to death. It is significant that the only dead fawn recovered that could be examined at a post mortem showed lesions consistent with death from heat stress.

It was concluded that the bulk of natural mortality in the Chinese Water deer was associated with the malpresentation of one or more of the foetuses in a single or multiple litter, and also from the direct or indirect effects of hyperthermia. The former would apply in any habitat, the latter was probably largely peculiar to this farmland environment. To this, in any habitat, must be added the chance abandonment of the young due to disturbance by dogs or people around the time of birth, and the death of the mother at this time.

Malpresentation can occur in any species and whilst it is not common, most herds have one or two deaths from this cause. Whilst in cases of birth difficulty the fawn is usually dead before any assistance can be given, this is not always desirable. Malpresentations occur naturally and the mothers mostly manage to expel the foetus. The stress of handling even tame deer is un-

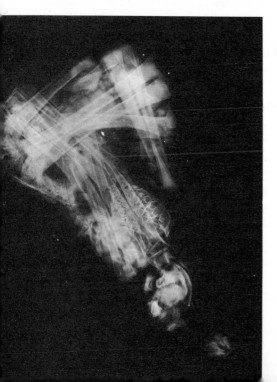

Fig. 11.1 Radiograph of the uterus of a Roe deer showing the retention of a foetus at least 6 months after its death. The consequences of such a condition in deer is not clear. This female was otherwise healthy and normal.

likely to improve the situation and attempts to deliver the foetus may well result in internal injuries to the mother, resulting in her death.

The majority of species known to me other than the Chinese Water deer do not have any specific perinatal problems that cause an unusually high mortality at this time. All are exposed to the hazards of appropriate natural predation from wolves, foxes, tigers, jaguars and similar predators, and there may well be years in which losses are particularly heavy from these causes. Most observers agree, however, that in most normal situations mortality at this time is not particularly heavy.

Care of the Young

In the period between birth and weaning, the fawn has to learn all that is necessary for its survival and it must develop and grow as best it can. The physical development and learning processes are part of play and there is a distinct sequence in which occur the different pattern of behaviour associated with learning. We will first consider the record of the care of the Chinese Water deer fawns and then look at how these and other deer are nourished and their physical development. We will then consider in more detail aspects of learning and the development of social behaviour in the Roe deer and other species.

Post-natal Care

On day three and thereafter, Pippa was suckling her fawns five or six times during daylight hours. This contrasts with Becky who fed her fawn infrequently. We saw it fed twice during daylight hours, although if the fawn were distressed—as for example by catching it to record its development—it was normally suckled by its mother. Pippa's fawns normally sucked together. They stood almost parallel to the mother so that their hind quarter were by her head. At first, they were small enough to stand underneath her. Whilst suckling, Pippa licked the fawn's anus or stood staring or eating. She rarely suckled the fawns when laying down. When sucking the fawns tugged and nuzzled the teats and udder and often struck the ground with their fore foot stiff and extended.

Pippa groomed the fawns frequently and payed particular attention to the anal region. This grooming of the anal region appears
to be very important in young fawns. In the first few days the
faeces passed are shapeless, yellow and sticky like egg yolk and
on one occasion we found a very inactive fawn whose anus was
completely gummed up. The later faeces (plant food is taken from
day 2) are firm pellets and the fawns are easily able to expel them.
Becky suckled her fawn for approximately four weeks and Pippa
for eight weeks. Pippa's fawns were weaned abruptly.

The milk of deer is very rich and nourishing. Like cows its
composition is thought to vary during lactation. In Table 11.1 are
several analyses of deer's milk, with those of some domestic
species for comparison. Unfortunately, it is not easy, particularly
from the smaller deer, to obtain a sample of sufficient size for
analysis by the techniques used in dairy laboratories and this is
why our knowledge of the composition of deer milk is so limited.

In the first few feeds, the fluid is only partly milk, the majority
being colostrum. The colostrum has many important functions in
priming the fawns' bodily functions and is generally regarded as
vital for the fawns' survival. Colostrum contains many large protein molecules associated with antibody protection of the young.
These molecules are too large to have crossed the placenta and
after a few days would also be quite unable to enter the fawns body
via the alimentary tract. For about the first day of life, the wall
of the gut will permit the passage of these huge molecules into the
blood system, after which the barriers go up and only small
molecules of food substances are able to pass through.

Recent work on Red deer at the Rowett Research Institute in
Aberdeen, Scotland (Arman, 1974) has provided quantitative data
on the composition and production of milk in animals kept in
close confinement. The maximum yield of milk was attained early
on in the lactation, with a yield of 1·4–2 kg (3–4 lb) per day. During
early lactation, calves suckled from ¾–4 minutes at a feed and took
from 150–630 g (5½–22 oz) of milk. In the first 150 days of lactation, the total milk production of well fed animals was 140–180 kg
(309–397 lb). In animals on a restricted diet, the yield was only 65
kg (143 lb). The composition of the milk altered during lactation
and early and late lactation analyses are given in Table 11.1.

Fawns are not suckled frequently under natural conditions, probably in early life not much more than once every 5–6 hours. The quantity of milk is quite small because it is so concentrated. It is a common mistake in hand-rearing to give diluted cows milk in large quantities, itself already too weak. The fawn's stomach is small and is not designed to cope with a large volume of fluid.

Table 11.1 Analyses Indicating the Major Constituents of Deer Milk with Comparative Figures for Other Wild and Domestic Species

Species	Total solids %	Fat %	Protein %	Lactose %	Comments
Fallow	25·3	12·6	6·5	6·1	
Sika	36·1	19·0	12·4	3·4	
Red	34·1	19·7	10·6	2·6	
Red (Rowett)	21·1	8·5	7·1	—	Average 3–30 days p.p.
Red (Rowett)	27·1	13·1	8·6	—	Average post 101 days p.p.
White Tailed	21·0	6·0	7·8	4·6	
White Tailed	—	15·1	11·9	3·7	
Mule	24·4	10·9	7·6	5·4	
Muntjac	29·7	15·9	9·2	3·8	Wild animal c. 10 days p.p.
Chinese Water deer	18·4	6·1	8·1	—	Wild animal 23 June
Roe	—	6·7	8·8	3·9	
Roe	25·7	11·9	11·5	—	Wild animal 9 October
Black Wildebeest	—	8·7	6·9	3·7	
Eland	—	9·8	7·6	4·9	
Musk Ox	17·4	6·6	8·1	2·3	Captive 14 days p.p.
Musk Ox	21·5	11·0	5·3	3·6	Wild animal 24 hrs p.p.
Cow	—	3·6	3·3	4·7	
Goat	—	4·5	3·3	4·1	
Sheep	—	11·9	6·1	4·8	
Pig	—	8·5	5·8	4·8	
Dog	—	14·8	16·0	2·9	
Man	—	3·5	1·5	6·8	

Within a few days, fawns are nibbling at soil and also experimenting with blades of grass. Chinese Water deer fawns are regularly taking solid food in 3–4 days. We believe that the eating of some soil may have two possible functions in the absence of the mother. It may firstly be an attempt to counter stomach acidity or it may be an attempt to acquire the micro-organisms which will form the flora of the rumen. Without this flora, digestion of plant materials cannot occur. These would possibly also be acquired by licking the mother, or from her grooming of the fawn. A third probability is that the soil may aid in the formation of firmer pelleted faeces, and the stimulation of peristalsis, to help the passing of the yolk-like excreta from the gut. Whatever its function, it certainly occurs in a range of species and appears to be very important.

The taking of plant food occurs quite early in the life of those species whose fawns we have seen reared, namely Red, Fallow, Sika, Water deer and Muntjac. This taking of grass positively precedes by as much as a week or more the first observations of active rumination, so there must be a good reason for this for the quantities taken are not insignificant. In hand-rearing, soil and grass and leaves are provided from day two.

Fawns grow rapidly in size, strength and activity. For this reason it becomes progressively harder, even in the ideal circumstances of captivity, to catch and weigh them. So much so, that if the staff are to have any future relationship with them, and injury to the deer is to be avoided, data collection has to stop. In the wild, it is not just the enormous problem of recapturing the fawn but of finding it again! We have been extremely fortunate with the Chinese Water deer to be able to weigh Pippa's and Becky's fawns in order to compare their development on the mother with fawns caught and re-caught in the wild also on their mothers. We attached great importance to this information as establishing a standard by which to judge the progress of bottle reared fawns. Of especial value also are the recaptures of wild Roe deer not only as fawns but again at various ages. This data from the work at Cheddington was kindly made available by Mrs. Francis and the UK Forestry Commission. This type of data is very hard to come by, and in many species there are no records at all of the progress

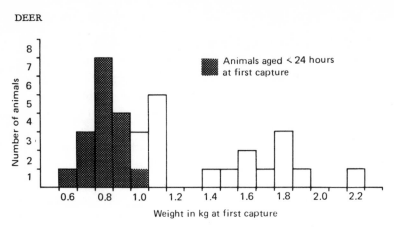

Fig. 11.2   The range of variation in birth weight of Chinese Water deer on the farm study area, southern England.

of either natural or artificial rearing of deer; it is most desirable that anyone doing this should keep records of food given and physical and social development.

There is considerable variation in the rate of growth between the fawns as there also is in birth weight; Fig. 11.2 shows the birth weight of Chinese Water deer captured on the farm. The average daily growth was calculated from the difference in weight between first and successive captures divided by the number of days. On the farm rates varied from 40 g (1·4 oz) measured over 10 days and 90 g (3·2 oz) measured over 8 days. The highest rates were found in the fawns reared by Pippa and Becky. Pippa's twin fawns averaged 140 g and 110 g (5 and 4 oz) over 9 days, and Becky's fawn 120 g (4·2 oz) over 18 days. It is probably significant that these higher growth rates were on mothers maintained throughout the winter on a very high plane of nutrition, both in quantity and variety, as compared with those on the farm.

From an analysis of weights of Roe deer at first capture, the perinatal weight average would seem to be represented by the weight category 1·8–2 kg (4–4·5 lb). Two fawns have been recaptured, one apparently a single male weighed 2·7 kg (6 lb) and over 8 days its growth averaged 120 g (4¼ oz). The second was a female of twins which increased from 2 to 3 kg (6·5 lb) over 9 days a rate of 100 g per day. On the same day as the last weight the male sibling was also caught and this weighed 3·2 kg (7 lb).

By the New Year, the Roe fawns born in May/June are in the 15–20 kg (33–44 lb) live weight range, compared to 21–26 kg (46–57 lb) in their second and subsequent winters. In the Chinese Water deer, growth is even more rapid, reaching 9–12 kg (20–26 lb) before the end of the year. In Fallow deer, average perinatal weights are about 4–5 kg (8–11 lb) and in their first year reach 19–32 kg (42–71 lb) in males, compared to 50–80 kg (110–176 lb) in males in their third year and older. Not only are the Fallow slower developing, but there is a great deal of variation in weights of adult males from place to place, depending on conditions. The Japanese Sika deer in southern England also has a similar pattern of development (Horwood and Masters, 1970). Perinatal weights are about 4·5–5·5 kg (10–12 lb) with calves reaching about 24 kg (53 lb) average in the first winter, thereafter adult females average about 39·5 kg (87 lb) whilst the males would appear to increase for several years to a mature weight of around 68 kg (150 lb). Accurate ages for the growth to maturity are not known except from antler estimates of age.

12 Behavioural Development of the Roe

In the White Tailed deer, Roe, Chinese Water deer and Fallow, for example, there is a prolonged period of postnatal contact between the mother and the young. Several days may be involved in establishing and fixing the more vital components of the bond. In Reindeer and to some extent also in the Moose the vital lessons must be learnt much more swiftly for the young have to follow the mother within a few hours of birth. The Reindeer calf will find itself caught up with many hundreds of other calves and adults in a lengthy and hazardous migration, and its survival will depend on its ability to maintain contact with its mother.

In the Roe, the learning is spread over a much longer period and below is a description of certain aspects of this period of development drawn from a study of these animals by Dr. Yngve Espmark (1969) in Sweden.

In the first few days after birth most of the contact between the mother and young was initiated by the mother. In the immediate post partum period, when the mother is laying with the fawn, contact was made by both the mother and the young. Later, when they were regularly separated, the mother returned to the fawn and, at first, would go right up to it, lick and nuzzle it and encourage it to suck. Later, she only approached the area where the fawn was lying and signalled it to approach and feed. About the middle of the second week, when the fawns were more active, the contact was made by the fawn, who would stand and call for the mother by loud 'peeps'—as a result of which the mother approached and fed the young. Towards the end of the second week this behaviour was much less often seen and the fawn would wander around seeking visual contact with the mother. That was the normal pattern for the next two months or so, at the end of which the behaviour of the fawn increasingly corresponded with that of the mother as they now kept company.

Fig. 12.1 Roe deer fawn approximately 2 days old showing the concealment behaviour of the young Roe.

The relationship between the fawn and its mother was very strong and the mothers were very intolerant of other females in the area of their fawns. Indeed, there seemed to be an area of about 1 hectare (2½ acres) which a doe would regard as her territory at this time. Whilst strange bucks were tolerated, females were not. Females approached by fawns other than their own were normally aggressive to them and would not allow the fawn to approach. Bucks, on the other hand, were much more curious about the fawns and although the fawns would often run away from a buck, aggression was very low key and as often as not the buck would also shy off.

This territorial imperative is also strong in Chinese Water deer, it certainly occurs to some extent in free living animals, but we observed it mostly in the relationship between Becky and Pippa and their fawns. Shortly before either gave birth, Becky became dominant to Pippa for the first time and would attack and chase her viciously, so that they had to be separated by a fence of wire, the male remaining with Pippa. Aggression continued through the wire and, following the birth of Pippa's fawns, it intensified. Whenever the fawns approached the wire Becky would fly at it trying to strike them with her feet through the wire. The male, in contrast, was interested in the fawns and would approach and sniff them and was entirely tolerant of them. Whilst the situation was an artificial one, the field evidence would suggest that it was only the intensity of the reaction that was different, rather than the occurrence.

Because of the territory, it is possible that the fawn, since it is looking for food, responds more to the shape or smell of its species rather than to a specific maternal smell, since in most cases it will be the mother that is contacted. It is interesting that it has been found possible to substitute Roe fawns between families and to have these adopted, provided that the fawns were not more than three weeks old. This is a much greater limit than in Chinese Water deer and probably most other species as well.

The number of visits to the Roe fawn varied between the families and the areas in which they were studied. In a large enclosure, Espmark (1969) found for three families that the number of visits was three per day and that the time spent was similar in two of them but different in the third family. A fourth family which he studied intensively in a much smaller enclosure visited on average, six times a day. This was almost certainly caused by the closeness of the fawn to its mother. Bubenik (1965), on the other hand, records 9–11 visits under more intensive conditions.

The care periods included both suckling and grooming and other social actions. It is interesting that the number of sucking attempts by the fawns declined over the first few weeks. At first, nearly all attempts were successful but in the second week fewer attempts were and thereafter there was rarely more than one attempt per visit and this almost always succeeded. The pattern of feeding tended to be an initial long feed followed by shorter subsequent feeds. This was longest at first when the first suck averaged about five minutes and $1\frac{3}{4}$ minutes for a second sucking period. It is interesting that as the fawn got older, so the duration of sucking declined. In the 10–19 day period, first sucking shortened to a little over three minutes and to about $\frac{3}{4}$ minute for subsequent sucks. In the 40–59 day period this had declined to a single suck of about $\frac{3}{4}$ minute.

The majority of the care periods even in twin births involved only a single fawn at any one time. The fawns, at first, did not associate and seemed to have no desire for mutual contact. During the first ten days the distance between resting siblings averaged 33 m, but after this the distance closed considerably and for the first time fawns were regularly found lying within a metre of each other—a pattern which increased. This increase in sociality is

Fig. 12.2 Roe deer with twin fawns about 3 weeks old.

interesting. It represents a positive stage in development from the initial period, in which some degree of aversion or perhaps apathy ensures the separation. There is little doubt that since the flight reaction to an approaching enemy has not yet developed and the fawn crouches instead, this dispersion will affect the hunting efficiency of predators like wolves (and scientists!) and help to ensure that the whole litter is not so easily found or killed.

The frequency of company with the mother increased with age so that by seven weeks about 50% of her time was spent with the fawns and at about three months they were in regular company. At first, in twin births, it was the mother with one or other of the fawns, but with age, all three were more often in company and at about 3–4 weeks, nearly half of the contact involves all three; thereafter all three were normally together. As the fawns came together more, there was a corresponding increase in mutual activities in the absence of the mother as well as in her company. In fact, the fawns spent more time with each other than with the mother, even though they were in close association.

A very interesting feature was the pattern of activity (feeding, grooming, moving, etc.) between mother and fawns. The mother's activity decreased as that of the fawns reached a maximum and they then continued at a similar level to each other. This occurred at about three months of age and is perhaps to be regarded as a highly important break, representing the passage from the junior to the sub-adult stage. In the wild, this would correspond with the month of September, which in many ways is a turning point in biological activity in the Roe year.

The function of grooming has a varying significance. In the first few weeks of life, grooming is intensive and often near continuous during care periods and suckling. It is directed to the body, genital region, head and neck. It is frequently to the obvious annoyance of the fawn. At this age, it is particularly associated with cleansing of the body and the maintenance of the coat. It will also have a reassuring and social aspect. The Roe from about 3–4 weeks, and the Chinese Water deer from about two weeks, are fully able to maintain their own bodily functions and there is a corresponding fall off in intensive grooming of the fawn by the mother, more often it is discontinuous. Subsequently, grooming of the head and neck develops as a mutual exercise between mother and young and between siblings, and this continues as a social activity thereafter.

Play is a term that is not satisfactorily defined by behaviourists, mainly because play as we experience it is a personal matter and we cannot understand play experiences of other species. Yet as mammals and individuals, we all recognise play behaviour as we understand play. Even if the mock fighting of cowboys and indians and other war games would not be regarded by us as the preparation for war, it certainly contributes to the development of all kinds of physical and mental agility and shapes our attitude to many things. We therefore expect in animals to find that play and exploration are a part of learning about the world, as well as satisfying other more personal needs. Play in the Roe, as in many other species, includes chasing, butting, exploration, mock fighting etc., and involves both the individual, the sibling and less frequently the mother. Many of these activities are associated with learning about the immediate environment and achieving mental and physical co-ordination and precision. It is interesting that these activities are comparatively rare in the Roe over about eight weeks and that play with components of adult sexual behaviour then becomes more frequent. Many elements of adult behaviour patterns are seen in the play of the older fawns but do not form a complete sequence. In our Chinese Water deer, similar elements of play were seen and this would involve either one, but increasingly both fawns, plus the father and mother, either as active participants in an ever-changing game of chase or as the centre objects about which to play. In Red deer, in which the young fawns come together as a part of the female herd, there is a great deal of group play and my limited observations suggest that this might also be a normal arrangement in the young of other social species. This is an interesting contrast in behaviour associated with the need to learn group social behaviour, rather than the more solitary kind seen in Roe and Chinese Water deer.

Play can occur at any time of the day, including night, but in the Roe is more frequent in the late afternoon and evening and generally follows a period of quite extensive care, suggesting that a feeling of well-being is a trigger to play.

13 Delayed Implantation

In Roe deer, most matings occur in July and August, but development of the conceptus is arrested in the blastocyst stage. In the winter, delay is terminated (nidation) and the blastocyst implants in the period November to February and the fawns are mostly born in May/June. As far as is known, the Roe is the only deer to show this phenomenon, which does, however, occur in a number of other mammals, e.g. the badger, grey seal, stoat, glutton and some marsupials. In the course of a study of reproduction in the Roe deer and the nature of delayed implantation in this species, a number of very curious features emerged. Information from many different sources was used in the study and the results and the conclusions are of some interest. The basis of the study is a collection of over 700 reproductive tracts from Roe deer killed in the British Isles by management staff in the open season from November–March, and a few animals killed later in the year.

A preliminary analysis of the distribution of foetal weights and the stage of pregnancy showed that nidation usually occurs between late November and late January in the south of England, and in northern England and Scotland it is approximately ten days later. More refined calculations are necessary to determine the exact dates and limits. Plotting of this data by region showed that there was an approximate date after which nidation appeared not to occur. In the south of England, this is January 25th; in northern England and southern Scotland, January 31st; and in northern Scotland, February 3rd. The numbers and dates on which animals in delay were recovered after these dates are given in Table 13.1. Approximately 7% of the animals killed after December 31st are in delay after the critical date. This includes animals killed in February, March and April.

The gross appearance of the uterus, ovaries and *corpora lutea* of animals in delay after the critical date is similar to that of animals in delay before that date.

These results indicate that there is either a critical date after which nidation does not occur, or that there is a discontinuity in nidation suggesting two breeding periods. It is necessary to consider further evidence before discussing these possibilities.

All authorities agree that the peak of rutting activity in Roe is in July/August and the peak of births is in late May/early June. It is well attested that in many areas there is a renewal of erotic and territorial activity in approximately 10% of animals some time in late Autumn. In Britain, most observers place it in October, but elsewhere on the continent of Europe it varies from October to December. Births also occur later than May/June. We do not have any figures for these nor do we know precisely when these late births occur. They are, however, a fact known to our stalkers

Table 13.1   Date of Death of Animals Containing Blastocysts after Critical Nidation Date and Possible Dates of Conception Calculated Therefrom

Date recovered		Earliest dates (day/month) of insemination calculated using:	
		Long delay	Short delay
January	26 (2)	31.8	2.11
	27	1.9	3.11
February	2 (2)	8.9	9.11
	4	10.9	11.11
	5 (2)	11.9	12.11
	9	15.9	16.11
	10 (2)	16.9	17.11
	12	18.9	19.11
	14 (2)	20.9	21.11
	15	21.9	22.11
	18	23.9	25.11
	19	24.9	26.11
	23	28.9	30.11
March	26	29.10	29.12
April	4	7.11	7.1
	12	15.11	12.1

and when shot during the winter these animals are termed 'poor or weak fawns'.

Prell (1938) collated the records of 21 controlled matings of Roe and showed that matings in July, August and September resulted in births in May and June. The matings reported by Prell were not carried out to determine the exact gestation period. However, 15 of these matings indicate the gestation period to within a few days. The gestation periods obtained from Prell's data are shown below against the time at which they occurred:

Matings in August/early September   mean 293 days
Matings in late September   mean 220 days

The matings in late September resulted in births earlier than for the other pregnancies (in early April) and the gestation period was much shorter. This suggests that these had a much shorter period of delay than the other animals. From the data for southern England, the duration of post delay gestation appears to be about 145 days (mean date of nidation January 1st—mean date of birth May 25th). Thus, the gestation periods of 226 and 215 for these late matings is unlikely to be the gestation period of a pregnancy without any delay in nidation.

Both of these matings were carried out at Frankfurt Zoo and in both cases the does were mated by the same buck in successive seasons. The breeding history was as follows:

Mating	Birth	Gestation
Doe A		
5/8/96	7/5/97	275 days
29/9/97	13/5/98	226 days
Doe B		
16/8/96	2/6/97	290 days
24/9/97	7/5/98	215 days

It is clear that with the later mating the gestation period was shorter.

Two further breeding histories quoted by Prell are of particular significance. About April 1st, 1933, a grown fawn (about 11 months) was mated and gave birth on August 28th, 1933:

| 1/4/33 | 28/8/33 | 150 days |

In 1936, the fawn from this mating was mated to the same buck from October 4th–6th and gave birth on March 6th, 1937:

| 5/10/36 | 6/3/37 | 152 days |

These are both late matings and again the gestation period is further reduced. The duration of pregnancy (150–152 days) is very close to the estimate of 145 days which does not include the several days between conception and the blastocyst stage. It is thought that these records establish the duration of a gestation period without delayed implantation and confirm the validity of the technique for estimating this. The mean value of the gestation period with delayed nidation following summer matings quoted by Prell is 293 days. The peak of rutting activity in Cranborne Chase in England is August 4th and the birth peak is May 25th (Prior, 1968). This indicates a mean gestation period with delayed nidation of 294 days. From the data given by Prior (1968) the broad limits of summer breeding may be set as July 1st–August 28th. There may, however, be more earlier matings than later ones and these limits are in no sense absolute.

From these results, it is seen that the mean figures indicate that pregnancy is divided almost equally between a period of normal foetal growth and a period of arrested development. More precisely, there are three stages (the mean calculated values of which are given below together with the values calculated for Prell's data), and these are the period from conception to the blastocyst entering the delay phase, the duration of delay and the post nidation duration of pregnancy.

	Calculated (Days)		Observed (Days)
		Delay	No Delay
Gestation	294	293	151
Post nidation	145	146	—
Conception-delay	5	(5)	(5)
Delay	144	142	(0)

The calculated value for the duration of pregnancy to the end of delay is 149 days (144 + 5 days). This value can be used to calculate the approximate dates of conception of the last animals to undergo nidation.

Region	Latest Nidation	Estimated Conception
Southern England	January 25	August 30
Northern England and Southern Scotland	January 31	September 4
Northern Scotland	February 3	September 7

The figure for southern England agrees with the field observations. These are not late matings as defined in relation to Prell's date and the normal length of delay was therefore used. It could, however, be argued that a shorter delay should have been used (about 80 days), in which case conception would have occurred at the end of October. It is suggested, however, that earlier matings are more probable as these would represent the tail end of the normal summer matings.

There were 21 animals that had not undergone nidation after the critical date. From Prell's evidence, these animals would be considered to have mated recently and be about to undergo a normal gestation period (without delay) of 151 days. This is not tenable, as there is no evidence of any nidation between this date and the beginning of March. This would not be the case if very late matings had occurred. Further, Stieve (1949) found that from October to December only a very few males had sufficient spermatozoa in the epididymis (the testes were inactive) to effect fertile matings at that time, and none thereafter.

Having rejected the possibility that these animals had recently mated, there are three reasonable explanations left:

1 These animals are in delay; conception occurred in the summer breeding period but nidation will not occur until next year, or the pregnancy will terminate in the next summer breeding period;

2 These animals mated late and are experiencing a shortened period of delay and will give birth in the summer;

3   These animals were mated late; they will experience a pregnancy with a delay period of the normal length and give birth
in late summer/early autumn.

The wider question is whether these 21 animals are merely
aberrant, or whether they represent a proportion of the population
that has a different breeding season. These animals form approximately 10% of the breeding population.

The earliest date on which these animals could have been in-
seminated may be calculated using the values for shortened and
normal gestation delay periods, 85 (80 + 5) days and 149 (144 + 5)
days respectively. The results are shown in Table 13.1. The use of
the earliest date implies that foetuses would have been visible a
few days after the date on which the animal was killed. There are,
however, no such specimens. With the termination of most
collecting on February 28th, these inseminations must have occurred at least five weeks later than the earliest calculated date. A
correction (add 35 days) might therefore be applied to these conception dates. The use of the shortened delay figure causes problems because of the alleged limited fertility of the males at this
time. The normal length of delay minus 35 days, however, gives a
range of conception dates from October 5th to December 20th,
in which most animals are mated in October and early November.
It will be noted that this correction necessitated by the results,
places all matings within the known fertile period of the male and
concentrates these within the period of the false rut, when about
10% of animals show renewed erotic behaviour. It is estimated
that the variant animals formed about 10% of the breeding population. This data would indicate a resurgence of breeding activity
in October, after a breeding discontinuity in September, following
the wane of the summer rut. Parturition from these pregnancies
would occur between July 27th and October 16th, but most would
occur within one month from July 27th, which is consistent with
the size of some fawns shot later in the year and the occasional
late births known to stalkers.

Although more work remains to be done on this material, all
the indications are that British Roe deer have two breeding seasons; one in July and August, the other in autumn, mostly during

October and November. These seasons are discontinuous. The later breeding season applies to about 10% of the breeding females and pregnancies from both seasons are of similar length. This does not deny the evidence of Prell that late matings may have a shortened period of delay, or even none at all, but suggests that these captive animals were influenced by factors different from those affecting our wild animals.

There are many evolutionary implications of this discontinuous breeding period and it must be highly significant that the length of delay is only a few days shorter than the duration of active foetal growth. It is interesting to speculate on how such a system evolved in the Roe in the first place and also as to the direction of evolution at this time. Is the Roe becoming an autumn or winter breeder or is it evolving away from this? Time will tell.

14 Health and Disease

By and large, the deer of temperate regions are very healthy animals in their own habitat. Without the benefit of veterinary medication they suffer fewer diseases and harbour less variety of internal parasites than domestic stock. Freqently, the parasite burden is better tolerated by the deer than by livestock. The health status of the subtropical deer is less well known.

The spectrum of parasites and diseases which can affect a species is very much a property of the environment. The nature of the terrain, the other mammals, birds and invertebrates present, the types and numbers of farm livestock and the quality of the habitat are particularly important. Because of their very complicated life cycles, many infective organisms are species or locality specific. Some of the strains of a diseases may not readily cross-infect another species, so that potential transmission from farm stock to deer and *vice versa* may not, in fact, be a significant risk. In many parts of the world, the relationship between the health of wildlife and of farmstock is of special concern. In the British Isles, for example, bovine tuberculosis has been virtually eliminated from the cattle herds and brucellosis (contagious abortion) in cattle is now being similarly reduced. Strict control measures have eradicated foot-and-mouth disease and, to date, quarantine regulations have kept the country free of rabies. In such a programme of disease control in farm stock, it is important to know whether the wildlife is also affected. So far, in Britain, it has been shown that the deer are not reservoirs of these diseases and there is thus no danger of re-infection of farm animals from the deer. However, the animal health situation varies greatly from country to country and even between regions. For this, and the other reasons given above, I am not going to discuss to any extent specific disease situations, except where these are well known and acknowledged.

To do otherwise would risk causing unnecessary fears through misunderstandings of what is an important and, at times, sensitive matter. Anyone concerned about the disease situation in wild or domestic stock should contact local veterinary officials and wild-life officers, so that proper tests and investigations can be made. No action should be taken until the results of such tests are known.

In an adequately nourished population, parasitism and disease are rarely a significant primary factor in mortality. The commonest cause of death in deer populations are:

1 Shooting (legal and illegal)
2 Road accidents and injuries received
  from accidents and woundings
3 Malnutrition and starvation
4 Carnivore predation
5 Disease.

Which order these are ranked in depends on the species and the locality. With malnutrition and starvation, there is the added effect of parasitism. It has been shown that deer in poor condition are predisposed to greater infestation by both external and internal parasites. The ultimate cause of death may result from the activities of the parasite, but it is the nutritional condition that predisposed the animal to this.

Despite the importance of considering the specific situation, valid generalisations may be made concerning the types of organisms which affect the deer and the nature of their action. Deer are afflicted by external parasites. These feed from the body of their hosts and include lice, ticks, nasal flies (bots) and deer flies (keds).

The lice are very small, only a millimetre or two in length. There are both biting and sucking lice, but it is the biting lice that seem to be the most numerous on deer. Because of their size, small numbers of lice are unlikely to have a serious effect on their host. However, the occasional very heavy infestations clearly have a debilitating effect and a great deal of irritation will also be caused by their activities. Sucking lice may also transmit diseases. In a careful study of the incidence of ectoparasites on Chinese Water deer, it was found that the abundance varied between populations.

Table 14.1   Relative Incidence of Ectoparasites Between
Parkland and Feral Populations of the Chinese Water
Deer in Bedfordshire, England in Spring and Summer

Ectoparasite	Mean index of abundance	
	Parkland	Feral
Ticks, *Ixodes* spp	1·5	0·22
Keds, *Lipoptaena* spp	1·03	0·56
Lice, spp not determined	1·27	0·44

The animals from the lower density population, which were in better condition, carried far fewer than the more dense population. Table 14.1 shows the relative frequency of each kind. The mode of transfer of these lice to the young is very interesting. The distribution of the lice on the mother's body was established. Providing that the infestation was not heavy, the lice were largely confined to the inguinal region, the relatively sparsely haired surface of the mammary gland, and around the face. Examination of fawns, following their initial grooming, revealed that, in most cases, three or four lice had been transferred to the fawn. It is significant that the lice on the mother are concentrated in just those regions that are in contact with the fawn.

Several species of tick occur on deer in different parts of the world and the same species are found on many other mammals, as well as on domestic stock. Ticks are blood- and tissue-feeders and are of major importance as vectors of animal diseases, because they have the ability to pass pathogens transovarially and to maintain and transmit them over long periods. The life cycle of the tick is complex and all stages can be found on the deer in considerable numbers.

Several species of deer fly or keds, *Lipoptaena* spp occur on deer. These are blood-sucking flies whose life cycle involves no other host. The flies which hatch from pupae on the ground then fly on to their host, where they burrow down between the hairs close to the skin. Once on their host, they lose their wings and for this reason it is unusual to find them winged on the deer. Their effect on the host is probably slight.

A number of deer are affected by species of Bot fly *Cephenemyia* spp which deposit their eggs or minute larvae around the nostrils. Subsequently, in their third stage, they develop in the nasopharynx as large grubs up to about 25 mm length. They leave the nose to pupate on the ground. The incidence of Bot flies varies from year to year but it is thought to be a very debilitating parasite of Black Tailed deer for example.

Deer may also be affected by the larvae (warbles) of the Oestrid insects, commonly known as warble flies. Many other species of flies cause irritation to deer, but are not parasitic on them.

The helminth parasites of deer affect the internal organs. Most are found living in the various divisions of the gut, but others occur either in passage to or in residence in other organs. There are quite a few species actually and potentially to be found in deer. Healthy populations carry comparatively light worm burdens, but these can become a major cause of debility and disease under adverse conditions. The significance of the parasite may vary between the species as, for example, with the worm *Pneumostrongylus* These worms migrate through the brain and spinal cord and lodge in the meninges. In the American White Tailed deer they do little harm, but in the Moose they cause a fatal paralysis. These worms are related to the lungworms which, particularly *Dictyocaulus*, cause heavy losses in many species of deer. These worms develop in large numbers in the lungs and bronchii and give rise to pneumonia conditions. Infestations can be at a high level and the resulting parasitic pneumonia is a major cause of death in Roe deer in Europe and Mule deer in the USA.

Many species of nematode have been recorded from the gut and some of these occur in domestic stock, others, however, are specific to the deer. Their significance varies a great deal but most healthy deer carry a few representatives of the group without serious harm. Commonly found forms are the small *Ostertagia*, *Trichostrongylus* and *Haemonchus* worms, which burrow into the wall of the abomasum. Other groups are found in deer but are not of major or general importance. These worms can cause both chronic and acute gastro-enteritis and outbreaks of this can occur in deer from time to time. In Britain in domestic stock, these worms are associated with severe debility, scouring, etc. These clinical signs do not, however, occur to any significant extent in free living deer. The Roe, Red, Sika and Fallow deer apparently have a high degree of tolerance. In central Europe, however, *Haemonchus* is a frequent cause of death in Roe and in the western USA they are a major mortality factor in Black Tailed and White Tailed deer.

Deer carry tapeworms in their own right and also act as intermediate hosts for some of the carnivore-infesting forms. This can be a public health problem, for one of these causes a serious disease in man—hydatid disease—in which the liver and the lungs may be seriously damaged. Both Black Tailed deer and Reindeer carry in the lungs the cyst stage of the bladder worm (the larval stage of a tapeworm). Infected lungs are eaten by wolves and dogs and the cysts develop into the adult tapeworm in the intestines. The cycle begins again with the excretion by the dog or wolf of the tapeworm eggs. These can be ingested, either by the deer or by humans, in whom they develop into bladder worms migrating to the lungs or liver, man as well as deer being an intermediate host of this species.

A parasite of great importance in both farm and wildlife species is the liver fluke. There are several species of liver fluke and in many areas, fluke may be endemic and give rise to both acute and chronic infestations. Death from this cause alone is not common in deer, but the fluke being a blood feeder is a heavy drain on an animal and the liver is frequently badly damaged.

Deer are potentially susceptible to many of the infectious conditions found in both wild and domestic ungulates. However, a disease that occurs in one species may not give rise to clinical symptoms in another. Thus, one species may act as a potential reservoir of a disease without harm to itself. Deer are susceptible to foot-and-mouth disease and an outbreak occurred in California in 1924 in which deer contracted the disease from infected cattle. The outbreak covered a wide area and over 22,000 deer, of which about only 10% were affected, were killed in the eradication programme. Fortunately, the eradication programme was successful and the disease did not recur. Had it become established in the deer, it would have been a very difficult and costly matter to maintain livestock which are disease-free.

Ticks are a major vector of infectious diseases between a great

Fig. 14.1 (*left*) Lumbar vertebrae of a Fallow deer showing lesions of the bone. The lateral processes of the vertebrae have been broken and have repaired out of line. The interarticular surface of the centrum is pitted and eroded and there has been deposition of additional bone around the edge of the joint and also around the edge of the articular processes.

Fig. 14.2 (*right*) Degenerative lesions of the interarticular and periarticular regions of the metacarpal and first phalange of both feet of a Fallow deer. Damage to these bones is so severe that they have collapsed and deformed. The primary cause of these lesions is not known.

variety of birds and mammals and are capable of transmitting a variety of organisms. In the British Isles ticks transmit the louping ill (encephalomyelitis) virus, tick borne fever and the protozoan red water disease. The two former have been found in deer in Britain. Many Scottish Red deer carry antibodies to louping ill but no clinical cases of the disease have been recorded.

Deer frequently show signs of injuries which have resulted in gross deformation of the bones. These arise most frequently from car collisions and from bullets. Broken bones are mended, but the deformations are considerable. They do, however, illustrate the extraordinary recuperative ability of healthy deer. Associated with

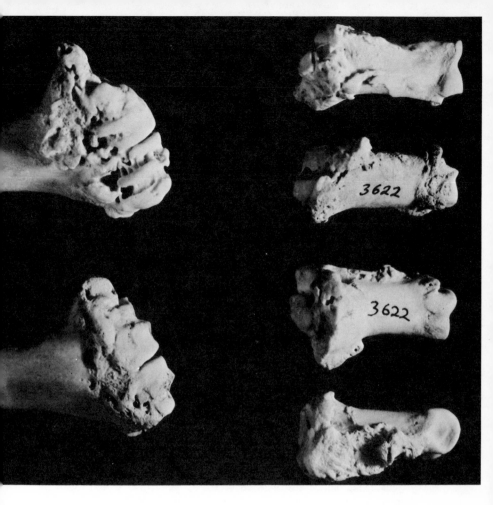

traumatic injury and probably also an infectious condition are various forms of arthritis. These lesions were studied in the Fallow deer by the writer. All the animals studied were killed in road accidents and many had previously been involved in non-fatal accidents. Bone lesions of one sort or another were the rule rather than the exception. These could be divided into two groups: those clearly resulting from physical injury (breaks, fractures, etc.) that had repaired to varying degrees; and chronic degenerative and proliferative lesions in the spinal column and limbs. The chronic degenerative lesions involved the erosion and deposition of bone on joint surfaces. This condition is localised in the spine where it involves the main body of the vertebra and the rib facets and also in the feet. On the ribs, it is the head and tubercle (which articulate with the vertebrae) that are affected. Lesions are found in the feet, from the lower end of the cannon bone into the hoof. Despite the fact that there is deformation of the articular surfaces, fusion of the bones involved is rare. Bony excrescences (exostoses) are found surrounding most of the joints of the fore and hind limbs and throughout the vertebral column.

In some animals, the periarticular exostoses are associated with other lesions of the interarticular surface. This would seem to be a secondary association resulting from the extent of the inter-articular degeneration and it is probable that the majority of periarticular lesions are not clinical. Although the incidence and severity of both types of lesions are greater in older animals, degenerative lesions occur in animals less than a year old. A selection of these are illustrated in Figs 14.1 and 14.2. The cause of these lesions could not be ascertained and there are a number of possibilities either alone or in combination that would explain them. How widespread these conditions are in other Fallow deer populations and also in other species remains to be determined. Some 50% of the Fallow deer in Epping Forest near London showed these lesions.

The condition of the teeth is of particular importance to the deer as damaged and broken teeth, or dental infection, can seriously impair the animal's feeding ability. In some areas, premature wear of the teeth can occur from grazing as a young animal on pastures contaminated with fluorine from industrial effluents. This causes softening of the teeth, which then wear rapidly and frequently become deformed. A common cause of dental irregularities in the adult arises from food particles wedged between the teeth, leading to an infection of the gums. This can extend to the bone and root of the teeth, causing abscess formation and, sometimes, loss of the teeth. Infections may also develop in the root canal. There are a number of oral infections, which like lumpy jaw (actinomycosis) in cattle, are caused by specific organisms. Deer are also susceptible to these, but superficially similar lesions may arise from other causes.

Free living deer are thus comparatively healthy animals and, in

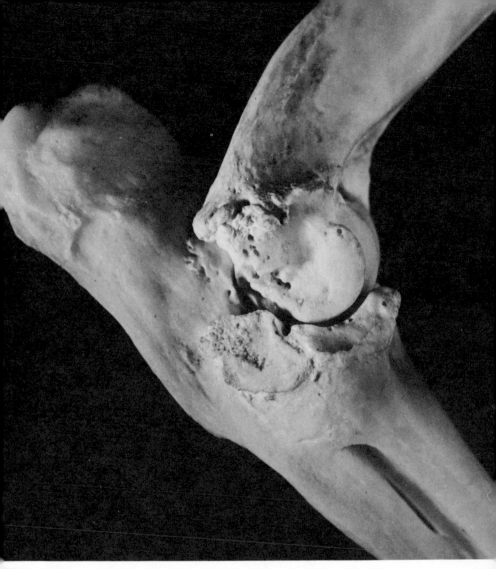

Fig. 14.3 Periarticular lesions of the elbow joint of a Fallow deer. There is both erosion and deposition of bone around the margin of the joint. At this stage no restriction of movement was apparent and there was no involvement of the joint surface. The further progress of the condition is uncertain.

general, are not a serious threat to the health of domestic livestock. With the advent of deer farming, it is likely that the disease and parasite situations will change and appropriate medication will be

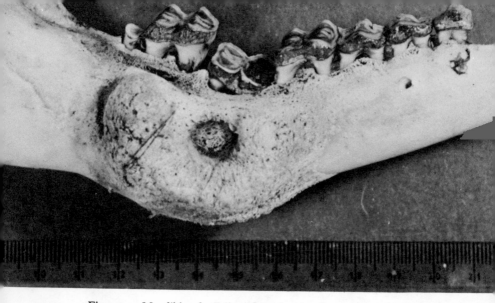

Fig. 14.4 Mandible of a Fallow deer showing 'lumpy jaw'. A condition similar in appearance to this specimen in domestic stock is called actinomycosis and is caused by a specific organism. Whilst this may also be the case in some deer, many of these arise from infections of the teeth and gum often caused by the impaction of abrasive foodstuffs.

a part of the management of domestic deer, and new diseases and conditions may well appear. In park Red deer, there is a condition known as enzootic ataxia which affects the nerve tracts of the spinal cord. The cause of this is not known but it is thought to be associated with a blood copper deficiency. This condition has not been observed in wild Red deer. Thus, veterinary studies of both wild and captive deer are of particular interest and relevance, not only for wild and captive management but also for conservation purposes.

Bibliography

Arman, P. (1974) 'Parturition and lactation in Red deer' *Deer* 3 (4), p. 222.

Banfield, A. W. F. (1961) 'A revision of the Reindeer and Caribou Genus' *Rangifer*. *National Museum of Canada Bulletin* No. 177.

Bannikov, A. G. (1975) 'Present status of the Bokharan deer (*Cervus elaphus bactrianus*) in the U.S.S.R.' Mimeo, 2 pp.

Bergerud, A. T. (1972) 'Food habits of Newfoundland Caribou' *Journal of Wildlife Management* 36 (3), p. 913.

Blower, J. H. (1975) Report on a visit to Pulau Bawean. Mimeo, 2 pp.

Bramley, P. S. (1970) 'Territoriality and reproductive behaviour of Roe deer' *Journal of Reproduction and Fertility*, Supplement No. 11, p. 43.

Bubenik, A. B. (1965) 'Beitrag zur Geburtskunde und zu den Mutter-Kind-Beziehungen des Reh (*Capreolus capreolus*) und Rotwildes (*Cervus elaphus*)' *Zeitschrift für Säugertierkunde* 30, p. 65.

Cambridge World Wildlife Study Centre (1975) 'Operation Hangul, 1974. Expedition to Kashmir.'

Chaplin, R. E. (1971) 'Some observations on the mating, vocal and territorial behaviour of wild muntjac deer' *Deer* 2 (6), p. 723.

Chaplin, R. E. (1972) 'The antler cycle of muntjac deer in Britain' *Deer* 2 (9), p. 938.

Chaplin, R. E. and White, R. W. G. (1969) 'The use of tooth eruption, wear, body weight and antler characteristics in the age estimation of male wild and park Fallow deer (*Dama dama*)' *Journal of Zoology* 157, p. 125.

Chaplin, R. E. and White, R. W. G. (1970) 'The sexual cycle and associated behaviour patterns in the fallow deer' *Deer* 2 (3), p. 561.

Chaplin, R. E. and White, R. W. G. (1972) 'The influence of age and season on the activity of the testes and epididymides of the fallow deer, *Dama dama*' *Journal of Reproduction and Fertility* 30, p. 361.

Cheatum, E. L. and Severinghaus, C. W. (1950) 'Variations in fertility of white tailed deer related to range conditions' *Transactions of the Fifteenth North American Wildlife Conference*, p. 334.

Coope, G. R. (1968) 'The evolutionary origin of antlers' *Deer* 1, p. 215.

Cowan, I. McT. and Holloway, C. W. (1973) 'Threatened deer of the world: conservation status' *Biological Conservation* 5 (4), p. 243.

Cowan, I. McT. and Holloway, C. W. (1974) 'Threatened deer of the world: research programmes of conservation' *Biological Conservation* 6 (2), p. 112.

Dagg, A. I. (1973) 'Gaits in mammals' *Mammal Review* 3 (4), p. 135.

Dansie, O. D. (1970) *Muntjac* British Deer Society.

Darling, F. (1937) *A Herd of Red Deer* Oxford University Press, London.

Dubost, G. (1970) 'L'Organisation spatiale et sociale de *Muntiacus reevesi* Ogilby 1839 en semi-liberté' *Mammalia* **34,** p. 331.

Dubost, G. (1971) 'Observations ethologiques sur le Muntjac (*Muntiacus muntjak* Zimmerman 1780 et *M.reevesi* Ogilby 1839) en captivite et semi-liberté' *Zeitschrift für Tierpsychologie* **28,** pp. 387–427.

Espmark, Y. (1964) 'Studies in dominance–subordination relationship in a group of semi-domestic Reindeer (*Rangifer tarandus* L.)' *Animal Behaviour* **12** (4), p. 420.

Espmark, Y. (1969) 'Mother–young relations and development of behaviour in Roe deer (*Capreolus capreolus*)' *Viltrevy* **6** (6), p. 461.

Frädrich, H. (1975) 'Notizen über seltener gehaltene Cerviden' *Zoologischer Garten N.F., Jena* **45** (1), p. 67.

Goodwin, H. G. and Holloway, C. W. (1972) *IUCN Red Data Book: 1 Mammalia* (2nd edn.) IUCN, Morges.

Goss, R. J. (1969) 'Photoperiodic control of antler cycles in deer. 1. Phase shift and frequency changes' *Journal of Experimental Zoology* **170** (3), p. 311.

Goss, R. J. (1969) 'Photoperiodic control of antler cycles in deer. 2. Alterations in amplitude' *Journal of Experimental Zoology* **171** (2), p. 223.

Grimwood, I. R. (1975) 'Field notes on the Calamian deer' (*Axis calamianesis*). Mimeo, 13 pp.

Hawkins, R. E. and Klimstra, W. D. (1970) 'A preliminary study of the social organisation of White Tailed deer' *Journal of Wildlife Management* **34** (2), p. 407.

Healy, W. M. (1971) 'Forage preferences of tame deer in a northwest Pennsylvania clear-cutting' *Journal of Wildlife Management* **35** (4), p. 717.

Henshaw, J. (1969) 'Antlers—The bones of contention' *Nature (London)* **224,** p. 1036.

Horwood, M. T. and Masters, E. H. (1970) *Sika Deer* British Deer Society.

Jungius, H. (1975) 'Report on the IUCN threatened deer programme in Argentina, Bolivia, Brazil, Paraguay and Peru'. Mimeo, 15 pp.

Lincoln, G. A., Youngson, R. W. and Short, R. V. (1970) 'The social and sexual behaviour of the Red deer stag' *Journal of Reproduction and Fertility*, Supplement No. 11, p. 71.

Markgren, G. (1964) 'Puberty, dentition and weight of yearling moose in a Swedish county' *Viltrevy* **2,** p. 409.

Martin, C. (1975) 'Status and ecology of the Barasingha (*Cervus duvauceli branderi*) in Kanha National Park (India)' Ph.D. Thesis, University of Zurich.

McCullough, D. R. (1974) *Status of Larger Mammals in Taiwan* Tourism Bureau, Taiwan, 36 pp.

McDonald, P., Edwards, R. A., Greenhalgh, J. F. D. (1971) *Animal Nutrition* Oliver and Boyd, Edinburgh.

Mitchell, B. (1970) 'The potential output of meat as estimated from the vital statistics of natural and park populations of red deer' *Deer* **2** (1), p. 453.

Morris, D. (1965) *The Mammals* Hodder and Stoughton, London.

Petocz, R. G. (1973) 'The Bactrian deer (*Cervus elaphus bacterianus*)' Report on the March 1973 Field Survey in Northern Afghanistan. Mimeo, 8 pp.

Pimlott, D. H. (1959) 'Reproduction and productivity of Newfoundland moose' *Journal of Wildlife Management* **23** (4), p. 381.

Prins, R. A. and Geelen, M. J. H. (1971) 'Rumen characteristics of Red deer, Fallow deer and Roe deer' *Journal of Wildlife Management* **35** (4), p. 673.

Prell, H. (1938) 'The duration of pregnancy of the roe deer' *Züchtungskunde* **13**, pp. 325–45.

Prior, R. P. (1968) *The Roe Deer of Cranborne Chase* Oxford University Press, London.

Ranjitsinh, M. K. (1975) 'Note on the Manipur Brow-antlered deer'. Mimeo, 4 pp.

Short, H. L. (1971) 'Forage digestibility and diet of deer on southern upland Range' *Journal of Wildlife Management* **35** (4), p. 698.

Soper, E. (1969) *Muntjac* Longmans, London.

Staines, B. W. (1974) 'A review of factors affecting deer dispersion and their relevance to management' *Mammal Review* **4** (3), p. 79.

Stieve, H. (1949) 'Anatomisch-biologische Untersuchungen über die fortpflanzungstätigkeit des europäischen Rehes (*Capreolus capreolus capreolus*)' *Zeitschrift für mikroskopisch-anotomische Forschung* **55**, p. 427.

Stonehouse, B. (1968) 'Thermoregulatory function of growing antlers' *Nature (London)* **218**, p. 870.

Strandgaard, H. (1972) 'The Roe deer (*Capreolus capreolus*) population at Kalø and the factors regulating its size' *Danish Review of Game Biology* **7** (1).

Taylor, W. P. (1956) 'The Deer of North America' Stackpole, Harrisburg and Wildlife Management Institute, Washington.

Thomson, B. R. (1971) 'Wild reindeer activity, Hardangervidda: July–December 1970' *Report from the Grazing project of the Norwegian IBP Committee, Trondheim.*

Whitehead, G. K. (1972) *Deer of the World* Constable, London.

Index